Calm and Sense is Common Sense

30 Life Lessons to Fulfillment

Sam (Ajit) Thiara

Copyright © 2025 by Sam (Ajit) Thiara

ISBN: 978-0-9937581-4-0 (Paperback Edition)

All rights reserved. No part of this publication, either writing or images, may be reproduced, distributed, or transmitted in any form or by any means, including photocopying, recording, or other electronic or mechanical methods, without the prior written permission of the publisher, except in the case of brief quotations embodied in critical reviews and certain other non-commercial uses permitted by copyright law.

All attempts have been made to verify the information contained in this book 'Calm and Sense is Common Sense: 30 Life Lessons to Fulfillment', but the author and publisher do not bear any responsibility for errors or omissions. Any perceived negative connotation of any individual, group, or company is purely unintentional. Furthermore, this book is intended for entertainment only, and as such, any and all responsibility for actions taken by reading this book lies with the reader alone and not with the author or publisher. This book is not intended as medical, legal, or business advice, and the reader alone holds sole responsibility for any consequences of any actions taken after reading this book. Additionally, it is the reader's responsibility alone and not the author's or publishers to ensure that all applicable laws and regulations for the business practice are adhered to. Any resemblance to places, events, or people is purely coincidental.

Published by Ignite the Dream Coaching and Consulting 2025
Cover by Whitney Law and Artist Design by Sam Kaplan

*This book is dedicated to my Mom and Dad—
Though you've left this world, your wisdom walks beside
me. Your legacy lives not in loss, but in the gifts you've
given me: lessons that light my path and life lessons
I now share with others.*

Acknowledgements

This book is a tapestry of countless conversations, insights, and shared experiences. To everyone who has sat across from me, sharing their stories and wisdom - your voices echo throughout these pages. Each conversation we've had has planted seeds that have grown into the insights shared here.

I owe deep gratitude to Sara Bordbar and Rachael Whyte, whose genuine belief in this project's potential to touch lives made it infinitely better. Your dedication and authentic input helped shape these words into something truly meaningful. Equally, Whitney Law has inspired me with her creativity and support where she designed the cover and back with Sam Kaplan.

To my closest supporters - my family: Sadhna, Ishaan, and Sahil, thank you for your patience with my writing adventures and for being willing audiences as I tested these life lessons. Your appreciation and understanding gave me the space to bring this book to life.

This book exists because of all of you and for that, I am grateful.

Table of Contents

Starting the Journey ~ An Introduction to Life's Lessons 1
Important Note ~ Preparing for Your Journey 5
Life Lesson 1 ~ You Are a Living Story – Embrace It! 9
Life Lesson 2 ~ Obstacles Are the Necessary Bricks on the Road to My Success 16
Life Lesson 3 ~ Beyond the Title: Realize 'Who' You Are – Not 'What' You Do! 23
Life Lesson 4 ~ Breaking Your Routine and Discovering the Extraordinary in the Ordinary 27
Life Lesson 5 ~ The Power of CARE: A Framework for Personal Growth 31
Life Lesson 6 ~ Change the World…From Impossible to Possible! 36
Life Lesson 7 ~ Overcoming FEAR: Focus on What I Gain, Not What I Lose 40
Life Lesson 8 ~ Stop Watching - Start Getting Busy: Never Be a Bystander in Life 46
Life Lesson 9 ~ Finding Control in the Uncontrollable with Agency 52
Life Lesson 10 ~ The Power of Transformation in a Transactional World 57
Life Lesson 11 ~ Your Big Dreams Start with Small Steps 62
Life Lesson 12 ~ Passion to Purpose: What Ignites You? 68
Life Lesson 13 ~ Mind Shift to Supporting Others: Are You a Bucket or a Candle? 74
Life Lesson 14 ~ As I Wander in Life I Wonder: Explore – Experience – Embrace 77

Life Lesson 15 ~ In a World of Critics,
              Be Someone's Champion............................79
Life Lesson 16 ~ Managing Others' Commitments:
              Clear Boundaries for Better Balance..........83
Life Lesson 17 ~ Intentions vs. Goals:
              A Path to Authentic Living.........................86
Life Lesson 18 ~ Change Your Words – Change Your World...89
Life Lesson 19 ~ Perceptions: Are they Truths or
              Just Our Own Personal Truths..................92
Life Lesson 20 ~ The 15-70-15 Rule:
              Don't Take It Personally............................95
Life Lesson 21 ~ Leadership Beyond the Title:
              A Life-Driven Approach 98
Life Lesson 22 ~ A Universal Truth: The More
              You Share, the More You Gain................103
Life Lesson 23 ~ The Beauty of Imperfection:
              Understanding Wabi-Sabi 106
Life Lesson 24 ~ Appreciative Inquiry: Unlocking
              Personal Growth Through Strengths.......109
Life Lesson 25 ~ The Truth Behind Imposter Syndrome:
              You Are Enough 112
Life Lesson 26 ~ Navigating Your Journey:
              Past, Present, and Future 116
Life Lesson 27 ~ Winning the Lottery
              but Losing the Ticket...............................120
Life Lesson 28 ~ Beyond Earning a Living:
              How to Truly Live......................................124
Life Lesson 29 ~ The Essential Outlet:
              How to Reconnect and Recharge.............128
Life Lesson 30 ~ You Are the Masterpiece:
              The Centre of Your Own Universe..........131
Bonus Final Lesson ~ Life's Hourglass:
              Making Each Day Matter 133
Conclusion ~ A Life Well Lived: The Final Lessons Learned ..135
Author Bio ~ Sam (Ajit) Thiara...............................139
Contributors ~ Whitney Law and Sam Kaplan...................141

"There is fear in me by sharing this book because of what people might think...but the bigger fear is what happens if I don't share and kept the words to myself!"

~ Starting the Journey ~
An Introduction to Life's Lessons

Are your days starting to feel like scenes from the same movie, playing on repeat? Do you yearn to infuse your life with deeper meaning? Is there a quiet voice inside you whispering that it's time for change?

We're all travelers on life's journey, but how many of us have stopped to check our compass? *Calm and Sense Is Common Sense* isn't just another self-help book—it's your invitation to pause. Not to halt your journey, but to ensure you're heading in a direction that truly resonates with who you are.

Through 30 carefully crafted insights, this book weaves together three decades of personal experience, hard-won wisdom, and transformative moments. It began with my own awakening—the day I chose to step away from being just another face in the corporate crowd to forge a path that felt authentically mine. Was it daunting? Absolutely. But in letting go of a role that merely fit my skills rather than my soul, I discovered something invaluable: my anchor points.

I call this common career trap "The Burning Tree Syndrome." Picture your job as a tree. When dissatisfaction sets in, it feels like your tree is ablaze. The natural response? Grab the nearest vine and swing to another tree—or in this case, jump to another job. Initially, the new position offers relief, but gradually, the flames of discontent begin to flicker again. So, you swing to the next tree, perpetuating an endless cycle of temporary solutions.

But what if, instead of seeking escape, you learned to extinguish the fire? What if you could identify the real source of your dissatisfaction and make decisions that align with your true calling? This is where anchor points come in—those non-negotiable values and principles that, like a climber's secure holds, guide you safely through life's ascent.

Most of us don't plan our careers; we stumble into them through a mixture of circumstance and convenience. We accept positions without questioning if they truly fit our values and aspirations. "Calm and Sense" offers a different approach. Through these pages, you'll discover how to identify your own anchor points and use them to navigate toward authentic success. We have taken many paths in our life, but the key aspects of this book are for you to now create your path.

Think of your current life as an off-the-rack suit. It might serve its purpose, but it doesn't quite fit perfectly. This book isn't meant to be rushed through—each lesson is an opportunity to tailor that suit to your unique measurements. By thoughtfully engaging with each insight, reflecting on its meaning in your life, and applying its wisdom, you'll begin crafting a life that fits you perfectly.

Following each lesson, you'll discover a thoughtful reflection prompt meant to help you internalize the wisdom shared. Having a journal or notepad nearby while you read would be valuable as it gives you space to capture your insights and explore how these principles resonate with your own life experiences. These moments of reflection serve as stepping stones, inviting you to not just read, but truly integrate each lesson into your personal journey of growth.

These 30 insights represent more than just lessons—they're stepping stones toward a more purposeful and fulfilling life. You will see overlapping ideas that continue to resurface throughout the book. Look for them as reminders of why you are starting this journey to transformation. That transformation is my gift to you, and it begins with the simple act of pausing to reflect.

"Your journey of a lifetime begins by each step. Take the first step!"

~ Important Note ~
Preparing for Your Journey

Instead of saying, "Okay, start reading and reflecting," it is important to have you prepare. Just like going on a trip, you need to pack and be ready to go. In this case, I want you to start thinking about an important concept that will be your road map moving forward throughout this book. Without your five anchor points (five is the right number to focus on as it provides enough of a solid foundation), the journey is just you moving forward without purpose.

Think of anchor points as your career's true north – they're the five fundamental elements that guide your personal and professional journey. Just as a ship's anchor provides stability in changing waters, these points help you stay grounded and focused while navigating the important decisions you face in life. They encompass your deepest values, natural talents, meaningful experiences, and core motivations that you are not willing to compromise.

This framework proves especially valuable during career transitions. Instead of jumping from one unfulfilling role to another, your anchor points help ensure each move brings you closer to meaningful work. They remind you that career success isn't just about skills and credentials – it's about creating a personal and professional life that reflects who you are and what you value most.

Your Anchor Points – Guide You and Not Bind You

Identifying your life's non-negotiable anchor points isn't as simple as drafting a quick list. It's a thoughtful journey of self-discovery that requires deep reflection and honest introspection.

Think of this process like creating a personal map - you're exploring the terrain of your experiences to understand what truly matters to you. As you navigate through this exploration, begin by examining your past. Reflect on the jobs you've held, classes you've taken, and social experiences that have shaped you. Ask yourself not just what happened, but how these experiences made you feel. What moments energized you? What situations left you feeling drained?

Dig deeper than surface-level observations. When you identify something you enjoyed, challenge yourself to understand why. Is it the type of work? The people you were with? The sense of accomplishment? These insights are the raw materials from which you'll construct your anchor points.

Don't get paralyzed by the fear of finding the "perfect" words. Your anchor points are living, breathing concepts that will evolve as you grow. They might be your values or ideals. They're not a rigid contract, but a flexible framework that adapts with you. The goal isn't to create an immutable set of rules, but to develop a dynamic understanding of what drives and fulfills you. At some point, realize the five anchor points and then pull them with you throughout this book and into your life. This will be a critical step in applying the 30 life lessons. At this stage, write down five words or a combination of words that resonate with you. For example, my five anchor points are: servant leadership, story sharing, activator/igniter, champion/enabler, creative collaborator. I hold these five very closely and these aren't just a collection of words, they are principles I live by every day.

Consider using assessment tools or seeking perspectives from trusted friends and mentors. Sometimes, others can see strengths and patterns in our lives that we might overlook. But remember, while external insights are valuable, the ultimate authority on your anchor points is you.

This is not about getting it right the first time, but about starting a conversation with yourself that will continue throughout your life. Your anchor points are a compass, not a chain - they're meant to guide, not restrict.

Reflection Question: Take a moment to write down five things that deeply matter to you. These can be anything - there's no need to overthink it or worry about getting it "perfect." This is just a starting point, and you can always revise your list as you continue through the lessons. The goal is simply to begin reflecting on what you value most.

Okay, now you can proceed to the first life lesson and embark on what is important to you…YOU!

"As you go through the pages, Relax-Reflect-Recharge"

~ Life Lesson 1 ~
You Are a Living Story – Embrace It!

To start your journey to fulfillment, I want you to embrace the following quote: "Everyone's life is an autobiography...make yours worth reading!"

Every moment you live adds another page to your personal autobiography. Take a quiet moment to reflect: Does your story captivate you? Are you crafting a narrative you'll be proud to look back on? If certain chapters feel incomplete or lacking in depth, remember that you hold the pen. Even small edits—tiny choices and minor adjustments—can transform your story's trajectory over time. Your autobiography isn't just a record of the past; it's the foundation from which your future chapters will unfold.

In the rush of daily life, we often forget to pause and appreciate the chapters we've already written. Our achievements, both grand and subtle, blur together in the constant forward motion of today. Yet your story deserves to be acknowledged and celebrated. Let this phrase resonate within you: "My life is an ever-evolving autobiography... I need to keep building it!" Make this more than a passing thought—let it become your guiding philosophy, returning to it regularly as you continue crafting your narrative. Your autobiography belongs to you - its reach is yours to define. Some find power in keeping their story as a personal compass. Others share it with family to deepen connections, while a few may feel called to touch a wider audience through publishing. There's no pressure to share beyond your comfort zone. The beauty lies in choosing what feels authentic to you, whether that means keeping your reflections private or letting them ripple out into the world.

Beginning Your Story

The first step in embracing your role as both author and central character is simple: create a space for your story to unfold. Whether you prefer the texture of paper beneath your pen, the familiar comfort of a journal, or the efficiency of a keyboard, begin capturing the depth of your experiences.

When you earned your diploma, degree, or certification, what obstacles did you overcome? How did they shape your character? As you navigate your career, which accomplishments fill you with genuine pride? If you find yourself in a chapter that feels stagnant or limited, perhaps it's time to introduce a new plot element: a hobby you've always wanted to pursue, an educational journey you've postponed, or an adventure you've only dreamed about.

Crafting Your Narrative: A Deeper Approach

Deep Reflections - Move beyond surface memories to explore the moments that truly shaped your story. Take time to delve into the pivotal experiences, people, and places that have contributed to who you are today. Here's how to enrich each element:

- **Recall the challenges that tested and strengthened you.** Reflect on the moments that pushed you to your limits—whether personal, professional, or emotional. What obstacles felt insurmountable at the time, and how did you overcome them? Consider the fears you faced, the setbacks you endured, and the lessons you took away. Ask yourself: Who did I become because of these experiences? How have these challenges built my resilience and shaped my values or anchor points?

- **Consider the relationships that altered your path:** Think about the people who have profoundly influenced your journey. Who believed in you when you doubted yourself? Who challenged your thinking or helped you grow? These could be mentors, friends, teachers, family members, or even brief encounters with strangers who left a lasting impact. Reflect on the role they played and how those relationships reshaped your priorities, choices, or worldview.

- **Celebrate achievements that surprised even yourself:** Look back on the moments where you surpassed your own expectations. These may be academic, professional, or personal milestones—big or small—that filled you with pride. What did you learn about yourself in those moments? Were there talents, passions, or strengths you hadn't fully realized? Celebrate these wins as evidence of your ability to achieve and grow, even when the odds felt stacked against you.

- **Revisit the places that left an indelible mark on your soul:** Reflect on the environments and locations that have defined chapters of your life. Was there a specific city, school, home, travels, or natural space that inspired transformation? Consider what these places represent—comfort, discovery, healing, or ambition—and why they resonate so deeply with you. Think about the memories tied to these places and how they contribute to your identity and story.

- **Time to journal:** To tie all these reflections together, create a timeline or journal entry that captures these key moments. Use a chronological or thematic structure to see how these experiences connect. What patterns or themes emerge? How do they reveal your personal growth, values, and purpose? By revisiting these elements, you can uncover a deeper understanding of your unique narrative and how it continues to evolve.

Discovering Your Theme

Following the points above, start viewing your life as an autobiography and out of this, you can begin to reveal the purpose of your story. Through thoughtful reflection, you might uncover the deeper significance of your journey or find inspiration to write entirely new chapters that align with your true calling. This is not about sitting down and building your life story in chronological order.

- **Personal growth and transformation:** Focus on what you have learned through your experiences. This is not about listing your educational resume and what marks you received but rather the important lessons you have gained. Knowledge is what we get out of textbooks, but instead focus on the application of the knowledge that has become your wisdom.

- **Professional evolution:** Think about how you have gotten where you are today. Not the simple step by step, schools or classes taken but more about the journey, those pinnacle moments, and what you have learned along the way.

- **Family bonds and relationships:** Expand further on the people who have made a profound impact on you and how. Was it something they did, showed you, or supported you on?

- **Creative expression and discovery:** Rather than the obvious lessons in life one learns, focus on anything that was out of the ordinary. Growing up, did you do an activity that you can now think about that helps you realize some values that emerged?

- **Resilience and overcoming adversity:** Not everything flows smoothly in life. Rather than overlooking them or ignoring them, let's face them head on because some of the most significant life lessons emerge from our setbacks. Think about situations that have tried to hold you down but you succeeded. How did you overcome the challenges? If you did not overcome a particular challenge, how did it help you get where you are today?

Embracing Authenticity

The most powerful stories emerge from truth and vulnerability. Don't hesitate to acknowledge the plot twists and challenging chapters—they're essential elements of your character development. Share your setbacks and victories with equal honesty; these are the moments that make your story genuinely human and inspiring. Remember, you're writing first and foremost for yourself.

The Ongoing Journey

Life is an ever-evolving story, filled with twists, turns, and chapters yet to be written. It doesn't have to be perfect to be meaningful. Each moment—whether a triumph or a stumble—adds texture to the narrative, creating a rich tapestry of experiences. Mistakes and imperfections are not failures; they are lessons, opportunities for growth, and reminders of our humanity. My story is still unfolding, shaped by the choices I make, the people I meet, and the dreams I pursue. It's a work in progress, just like me—a reminder that the journey matters more than the destination.

~ LIFE LESSON I ~

Remember: You are a living story, and never feel that your journey is insignificant or lacks importance to consider. Your thoughts are for you, or you can share with who you like. The most important thing is that you acknowledge that your life is something worth capturing.

Reflection Question: What are the standout chapters in your autobiography so far? Take time to list your proudest achievements and most meaningful moments. These can be headers or paragraphs you jot down. You can build on this later. Let these remind you of the story you've already written and inspire the chapters yet to come.

"What is the last story you read? What is the last story you told? What is the last story you lived?"

~ Life Lesson 2 ~
Obstacles Are the Necessary Bricks on the Road to My Success

I recently encountered someone struggling with their first major career setback - being let go from their job. Their experience highlighted an important truth: while we may wish for a smooth journey through life, setbacks and obstacles are not just inevitable, they're essential for our growth. One can mourn the loss of a job, promotion or project, but it is important to not dwell on the negative emotions that might arise.

Think about it: how can we truly appreciate success without experiencing setbacks? How do we develop problem-solving skills without facing challenges? While it's natural to hope for an easier path, these moments of difficulty are precisely what forge our resilience and character. View obstacles as growth opportunities rather than roadblocks, because obstacles teach us patience, persistence, and problem-solving skills. Consider how each challenge can expand your skillset or deepen your understanding of yourself and the world around you. By reframing obstacles as chances to grow, you empower yourself to turn adversity into advantage.

The key lies in how we approach these challenges. Here's how to transform obstacles into opportunities:

- **Shift your perspective**: Life's challenges can feel overwhelming but changing how you see them can transform your experience. Instead of viewing obstacles as permanent barriers, see them as stepping stones for growth.

    ○ Ask yourself: "What can this teach me?" and "how might this experience make me stronger?" Questions are powerful tools for introspection. When faced with difficulties, pause to reflect on the lessons hidden within. What can you learn from the situation that could prepare you for the future? Perhaps it's a new skill, a deeper level of self-awareness, or a greater capacity for empathy. Use these questions as a guide to navigate challenges with purpose and intention.

- **Focus on what's within your control**: When problems arise, it's easy to feel helpless or overwhelmed. Shift your energy toward the aspects you can influence, such as your actions, responses, and mindset. Recognize that some factors are beyond your control and letting go of those will free up energy to direct toward more productive efforts.

- Identify which aspects of the situation you can influence. Every challenge has variables you can impact. Determine where your efforts will be most effective and focus there. Whether it's your attitude, preparation, or communication, your proactive choices can create momentum, even in difficult circumstances.

- Let go of factors beyond your control to preserve your energy. Worrying about what you cannot change only drains you. Instead, channel your focus into constructive actions. Acceptance of the uncontrollable isn't surrender; it's wisdom. By understanding what you cannot influence, you make space for clarity, progress, and peace of mind.

- **Develop a strategic approach**: Facing challenges without a plan can feel like trying to drive a car with no steering wheel. Create a roadmap by breaking down overwhelming problems into smaller, actionable steps. Define clear goals, prioritize tasks, and identify resources you can leverage to tackle the situation methodically and confidently.

  - Break down challenges into smaller, manageable steps. A large challenge often feels impossible until you dissect it. Focus on one small step at a time, building momentum and celebrating progress. Each completed step boosts your confidence and brings you closer to a solution.

- Generate practical solutions. Brainstorm options to address your challenge and weigh their feasibility. Consider short-term fixes and long-term strategies and be willing to adjust as circumstances evolve. Solutions don't have to be perfect—they just need to move you forward strategically.

- **Identify when and whom to ask for help**: Recognizing when you need assistance is a sign of strength, not weakness. Identify people in your network—mentors, friends, colleagues—who can offer guidance, resources, or fresh perspectives. Asking for help opens doors to solutions you may not have considered alone.

  - Leverage your support network. You don't have to face life's challenges alone. Reach out to those you trust. Sometimes, just sharing your thoughts can provide relief, while their insights can help you see solutions you might have missed.

- **Build resilience**: Life's challenges will test you, but each one is an opportunity to strengthen your mental and emotional endurance. Building resilience means embracing discomfort without allowing it to overwhelm you and finding ways to grow stronger in the process.

- Draw strength from past successes and obstacles you have overcome. Remind yourself of the strength and resourcefulness you demonstrated in those moments. Trust that the same qualities will carry you through current and future difficulties.

- Remember that setbacks aren't failures; they're opportunities to learn, adapt, and grow stronger. Every setback carries valuable lessons. Instead of dwelling on what went wrong, focus on what you can take away. Use failures as fuel to refine your approach and keep moving forward.

- **Welcome fresh perspectives that might reveal overlooked solutions**: Others often see what you cannot. Invite feedback or ideas from people with different experiences and viewpoints. A fresh perspective can open your mind to alternative paths forward.

- **Practice gratitude and self-care**: Amid challenges, it's easy to lose sight of what's going well. Don't be hard on yourself. Practicing gratitude helps you maintain perspective, while self-care ensures you have the energy and resilience to keep pushing forward.

  - Maintain perspective by acknowledging what's going well in your life. Take a moment to reflect on the positives, even in difficult times. Gratitude shifts your mindset from scarcity to abundance, reminding you of the resources, people, and opportunities already present in your life.

- Practice self-compassion by replacing negative self-talk with understanding and kindness. Treat yourself with the same kindness and encouragement you would offer a friend. When you make a mistake or face setbacks, resist the urge to be overly critical. Instead, acknowledge your efforts and remind yourself that growth is a lifelong process.

- Prioritize self-care through meditation, mindfulness, or other grounding practices. Caring for yourself isn't indulgent—it's essential. Whether through mindfulness, exercise, or creative outlets, find practices that recharge your mind and body, enabling you to face challenges with clarity and strength.

Remember: Every obstacle you face is developing your resilience, problem-solving abilities, and emotional intelligence. While challenges may never be comfortable, they are instrumental in shaping who you become.

Reflection Question: Consider a past or current obstacle in your life. How might you apply these principles to not just overcome them, but to grow stronger through the process?

"If you don't experience sadness, how can you appreciate happiness?

If you don't encounter setbacks, how will you know you have succeeded?

If you don't risk...then how do you even know you have lived?"

~ Life Lesson 3 ~
Beyond the Title: Realize 'Who' You Are – Not 'What' You Do!

"I am not defined by what I do; I am defined by who I am."

In professional settings, we often default to introducing ourselves through our job titles or industry roles. While this is conventional, it barely scratches the surface of who we truly are. The real magic happens when we share the deeper purpose that drives our work and choices.

Consider this transformation: Instead of saying "I'm a marketing director with ten years of experience," try "I help businesses tell authentic stories that connect meaningfully with their audiences because I believe in the power of genuine communication." This shift from what you do to why you do it creates more meaningful connections and conversations.

Our professional titles are just headers in our larger story or autobiography. Each of us carries a unique combination of passions, values, and experiences that shape who we are. When someone asks what you do, consider sharing your essence rather than just your role.

For example: "I'm a collaborator who brings people together, a creative problem-solver who finds innovative solutions, and a lifelong learner passionate about sharing knowledge with others."

This approach reveals your authentic self and naturally invites deeper conversations. It moves beyond the constraints of job titles to showcase your true impact and purpose.

Understanding and expressing who you are begins with these key steps:

- **Explore your core values (anchor points)** - Identify the principles that guide your decisions and actions. Maybe this is a good time to look at the words you wrote down at the outset as potential anchor points. These become your foundation for authentic living. Do the anchor points start to align to you and how they might become your base? They will refine over time as you grow as an individual or even as you go through these pages, but very few people can describe their values because they are transfixed on their title.

- **Uncover your passions** - What activities make you lose track of time? What topics spark your curiosity and enthusiasm? These passions often reveal your true calling. By focusing on the activities that you appreciate, understand that they come naturally to you.

- **Recognize your strengths** – You can use tools like personality assessments to discover your natural talents. More importantly, reflect on when you feel most capable and energized. There are various tools available, such as 'High5 Test' that provide you with five key words. It is a valuable starting point in discovering your authentic self based on the 'High5 Test' - a free online assessment that reveals your five core strengths. Taking this test can illuminate aspects of your character you may not have fully recognized, offering a foundation for deeper self-understanding. Consider these five descriptors as initial brushstrokes in painting the fuller picture of who you are, and reflect on how deeply they resonate with your self-perception. Once you do the 'High5 Test', compare them to the anchor points you started with. Is it time to replace any of your anchor points with the 'High5 Test' results?

- **Create meaningful connections** - Align your anchor points, values, passions, and strengths to discover opportunities that resonate with your authentic self. By doing this, you will find those who have mutual connections to you and can support your personal development.

- **Seek external perspective** - Ask trusted friends or colleagues to describe your essence. Their insights often illuminate qualities we overlook in ourselves. It is helpful to reach out to those who know us best to get an understanding of some of the key descriptors of who we are.

Remember: Your identity is far richer than any job title. By understanding and embracing who you truly are, you create opportunities for deeper connections and more meaningful impact in everything you do.

Reflection Question: Do the 'High5 Test' and take a moment to reflect: Who are you beyond your professional role? Compare your 'High5 Test' results and your anchor points. At this stage, maybe create an interesting and engaging phrase to identify who you are based on what you do.

"Who are you? You are the eternal elements: Fire - the passion that ignites your purpose. Water - the calmness that flows through your spirit. Air - the energy that propels your days. Earth - the foundation that keeps you grounded through life's storms."

~ Life Lesson 4 ~
Breaking Your Routine and Discovering the Extraordinary in the Ordinary

Life often becomes a blur of routines, pulling us into autopilot where we simply go through the motions. Days merge, leaving us wondering where time went and what we truly accomplished. But within this seeming mundane exists countless opportunities for wonder and meaning—if we know how to look.

The key isn't making dramatic life changes, but rather taking small, intentional steps to enrich our daily experience. Whether it's committing to your health through exercise, exploring a new hobby, or rediscovering an old passion, these mindful choices can transform ordinary days into meaningful experiences.

Let's explore **CARPE**, that emerged out of my first TEDx talk on storytelling called: 'Discovering the Extraordinary in the Ordinary'. A simple and effective method based on five words that create a process: Curiosity - Appreciation - Reflection - Perspectives - Experiences for uncovering the extraordinary in everyday moments:

Curiosity – definition - a strong desire to know or learn something.

Be an explorer in your own life. Take a different route home, pause to examine something that catches your eye, or engage your senses fully in a familiar environment. Like noticing a peaceful stream during your walk, curiosity invites you to stop, sit and truly experience what's around you.

Appreciation – definition - recognition and enjoyment of the good qualities of someone or something.

Once curiosity draws you in, practice genuine gratitude for the moment. Notice how "enjoyment" contains "joy" at its core—a reminder that appreciation opens the door to finding delight in simple pleasures. When you quiet your mind and truly observe, even a gentle stream can become a source of profound peace as you sit on the shore.

Reflection - definition - a quiet and serious thought process resulting in deeper understandings.

Ask yourself, "What does this mean to me?" This is where meaning emerges. Perhaps you notice a leaf floating downstream and this might reveal insights about your own life's journey, your lack of control in your life at this stage with the stream carrying the leaf. Reflection transforms observation into understanding which happens as you think deeper about what you are experiencing.

Perspectives – definition - a particular attitude toward or way of regarding something; a point of view.

Your unique experiences and viewpoints give depth to these moments of reflection. The perspectives you hold align to the reflections you have encountered. What seems ordinary to others might hold special significance for you based on your personal journey. Your perspective turns simple observations into meaningful insights.

Experience – definition - practical contact with and observation of facts or events.

This final step brings everything together through action. Without it, insights remain just thoughts and never get realized. When a moment reveals something important—like recognizing the need for change—take concrete steps to honor that insight and capture it. This might be through journalling, writing a note on your phone that you can expand on later or sharing the moment with someone else.

Remember: Every ordinary moment holds the potential for extraordinary discovery. By approaching life with intentional awareness, we transform routine into revelation, finding wisdom and wonder in the everyday flow of life.

Reflection Question: Try this - Choose something ordinary from your day: an occurrence in your day, or even a familiar object on your desk. Look at it and apply the CARPE process: What draws your **Curiosity** about it? What can you **Appreciate** in this moment? What deeper meaning emerges when you **Reflect**? How does your unique **Perspective** influence your understanding? What action can you take based on this insight to make it an **Experience**?

"Seek out your adventure. Adventures won't seek you."

~ Life Lesson 5 ~
The Power of CARE:
A Framework for Personal Growth

When asked if we care, our immediate response might be, "Of course I care!" We think about our families, our work, our communities - all the things that matter to us on a personal level. While this natural caring is vital, there's a deeper dimension to care - one that can transform how teams function, organizations thrive, and societies evolve. Take the word care and now transform it into a concept called CARE.

CARE isn't just an emotion; it's a dynamic process that reaches beyond individual concern into the realm of collective impact. It's a framework that can reshape how we approach challenges, interact with others, and create lasting positive change.

In this case, CARE represents four words that are a must have in our lives. When all four are activated, it will provide qualities in building stronger relationships, enhancing personal growth, and creating meaningful impacts in communities and organizations. The words are basic and simple, but when combined, these words provide an underlying significance that enables us to accomplish great things.

Few concepts are as transformative as **CARE: Collaboration – Adaptability – Resilience – Empathy**. This framework isn't just about individual qualities; it's about how these elements work together to create a foundation for personal and professional growth. Each one of these words layer into each other to create a compelling process for your personal and professional growth.

Understanding CARE

1. **Collaboration** - The heart of human achievement lies in working together. When we collaborate, we tap into collective wisdom, share diverse perspectives, and achieve what would be impossible alone. It's not just about teamwork - it's about creating environments where ideas flourish and innovation thrives through shared purpose. We don't have all the answers and the ability to solve all the problems so we find support in others.

2. **Adaptability** - In our rapidly changing world, adaptability has become crucial for success. It's the ability to pivot when circumstances shift, embrace new approaches, and stay flexible in the face of change. Adaptable individuals don't just survive change - they use it as a catalyst for growth.

3. **Resilience** - Life inevitably presents challenges, but resilience determines how we respond to

them. We might be on a journey with others. How are we preparing and embracing the journey? It's the inner strength that helps us bounce back from setbacks, learn from failures, and keep moving forward. Resilience isn't about avoiding difficulty - it's about growing stronger through adversity.

4. **Empathy** - The cornerstone of meaningful relationships, empathy enables us to truly understand and connect with others. It goes beyond simple understanding to create genuine connections, foster trust, and build communities where everyone can thrive. In simple terms, how are you looking after the people around you?

The Synergy of CARE

What makes CARE powerful is how these elements reinforce each other. **Collaboration** becomes more effective when paired with **Empathy** because it is about caring for those around us. **Adaptability** strengthens **Resilience** as a result of being flexible and agile. **Resilience** grows through **Collaborative** support. **Empathy** enhances our ability to **Adapt** to others' needs.

This interconnected nature creates a positive cycle:

- **Collaboration** provides the support needed to face challenges.

- **Adaptability** gives us tools to navigate change and such challenges when we feel supported by Collaboration.

- **Resilience** helps us persist through difficulties as we are adaptable and supported by Collaboration.

- **Empathy** ensures we grow together rather than alone as we focus on the journey with Collaboration, Adaptability and Resilience.

Remember: CARE isn't just a framework, it's a pathway to building stronger relationships, facing challenges with confidence, and creating a more meaningful life. By embracing these qualities, we don't just improve ourselves; we contribute to building stronger, more supportive communities.

Reflection Question: Think about significant moments in your life where you demonstrated each aspect of **CARE**:

- When did collaboration lead to an achievement you couldn't have reached alone?

- How has adaptability helped you navigate unexpected changes?

- What challenges has your resilience helped you overcome?

- When has empathy allowed you to make a meaningful connection or difference in someone's life?

"If you try, you can have the ability to achieve. If you don't, you only have the shadows of what might have been."

~ Life Lesson 6 ~
Change the World...From Impossible to Possible!

We all start with dreams of changing the world. As children, we envision grand gestures and sweeping transformations that will leave a lasting mark on humanity. But as life unfolds—as we navigate careers, build families, and shoulder responsibilities—these ambitious aspirations often fade into the background. The world seems too vast, too complex for one person to influence. Overwhelmed by its immensity, we retreat into our daily routines, letting those early dreams slip away.

Yet perhaps we've been looking at it wrong all along. The key isn't to abandon our desire for change, but to shift our perspective. When we view the world only through our own lens, every challenge appears too big a challenge and impossible. But when we focus on the tangible differences we can make in individual lives, we discover that meaningful change is not only possible—it's happening every day and maybe you may not realize how you have changed the world.

~ LIFE LESSON 6 ~

Let me share a story that transformed my understanding of what it means to change the world.

While volunteering at an employment assistance organization, I met Robert and his wife over tea. Their story was one of mounting struggles—both unemployed, they were finding it increasingly difficult to provide for their 10-year-old daughter, who had had to sleep on the floor due to their meager apartment. As they shared their circumstances, their despair was noticeable. They felt abandoned by a system that seemed to offer little support.

During our conversation, I spoke words that would prove more impactful than I could have imagined: "No one is going to rescue you. You have to pull your energy together and help yourselves and I will do what I can." We parted ways that day, and I left their resumes with the organization, hoping they might find their way forward and never saw them again.

Years later, while serving on a non-profit board, I spotted Robert in the crowd. He approached me with a warm embrace and an apology for not sharing their story sooner. He said, those words—"No one is going to rescue you, and you have to help yourself had ignited something within us both". They had found the strength to secure not just one contract, but two. "Both of us are much better now," he shared with pride. "Our lives have changed, and we can provide for our daughter. She's doing very well, and we're doing well too. Our world has come back together."

That last phrase—"our world has come back together"—crystallized a profound truth within me: changing the world isn't about orchestrating massive transformations. It's about touching individual lives and helping others build their worlds in ways that matter to them. We don't need to impose our vision of what their world should be; we simply need to help them create the change that's right for their journey.

The path to meaningful change begins with simple actions: perhaps a conversation with someone in need, mentor someone who could benefit from your experience, join a non-profit organization that resonates with your values, or simply be that compassionate presence in your community. Each small act creates ripples that extend far beyond our immediate view, and you change the world through the eyes of those you help and you may never realize the true impact you have made.

Remember: It is not about changing the world through your eyes. Change the world through the eyes of the people you help and if they see the world differently, you have actually changed the world.

Reflection Question: How can you get involved in your community and make a positive impact? Think of your own way of making change. Consider the unique gifts and experiences you bring and think about how they might help others rebuild their worlds. This might be a good time to focus on the anchor points you are building as a foundation.

~ LIFE LESSON 6 ~

*"I look at the world in wonder.
I am here for a reason.
What is my purpose?"*

~ Life Lesson 7 ~
Overcoming FEAR: Focus on What I Gain, Not What I Lose

One of life's most paralyzing emotions is the fear of regret. It whispers warnings about missed opportunities and wrong turns, urging us to stay safely within our comfort zone. But regret isn't reality—it's a mental construct that exists solely in our minds. Once we allow it to take hold, it becomes a self-imposed prison, constantly reminding us of perceived mistakes and limiting our potential for growth.

Consider someone contemplating a career change. Fear creeps in, questioning their judgment: "Am I making the right choice? Am I qualified enough? What if I fail?" These doubts multiply like echoes in an empty room, drowning out the voice of possibility with concerns about what might be lost. This inner dialogue can prevent us from taking actions that could lead to profound personal and professional growth. We become paralyzed.

~ LIFE LESSON 7 ~

FEAR: A New Perspective

Rather than letting fear control our decisions, let's reframe FEAR as an acronym: **Forget Everything About Regrets**. This mindset shift encourages us to acknowledge regret without becoming its prisoner. While it's natural to consider what we might leave behind, we shouldn't let these thoughts prevent us from moving forward.

Picture yourself at a fork in the road—perhaps choosing between the security of an established career and the uncertain path of entrepreneurship. Standing at this junction can feel paralyzing; the fear of choosing wrong can keep us rooted in place. Yet remaining stuck, afraid to choose either path, is often the worst decision we can make because opportunities do not last forever. Equally unwise is rushing forward without thoughtful consideration.

Once we choose a path and begin walking, there's often a temptation to constantly look back, wondering about the road taken and if it is right or the path not taken and what is given up. This backward focus drains energy that could be spent embracing and enriching our chosen journey. While it's natural to occasionally wonder about alternative paths, our primary focus should be on maximizing the opportunities before us and focus on what you have gained and not what you have given up.

Practical Strategies for Overcoming Regret

Here's how to transform regret into a catalyst for growth:

- **Acknowledge and release**

  o Accept your feelings of disappointment or frustration—they're natural responses to perceived loss. Give yourself space to process these emotions, but don't build a home in them. Acknowledgment without dwelling is key.

- **Reframe your perspective**

  o Shift your focus from loss to gain by asking: how has this situation clarified what I truly want, and what unexpected opportunities have emerged from this path?

- **Return to your anchor points**

  o Remember the core values and principles we discussed earlier—your anchor points. Let them guide you forward with renewed confidence and clarity when you compare the opportunity to what really matters to you.

- **Embrace the trade-offs**

  o Every choice involves trade-offs. The opportunity you declined may have created space for something equally valuable in your life. Consider creating a thoughtful pros-and-cons list to make more rational decisions when facing future choices.

~ LIFE LESSON 7 ~

- **Focus on your circle of control**

    - Channel your energy toward what you can influence rather than dwelling on unchangeable circumstances. Transform regret's paralyzing effect into motivation for positive action.

- **Seek new opportunities**

    - Remember that opportunities aren't scarce—they're abundant. While you can't replicate exact situations, you can discover new paths that lead to equally meaningful destinations.

- **Build your support network**

    - Share your journey with trusted friends, mentors, or counselors. Their fresh perspectives can help you process regret and make more confident decisions.

- **Take decisive action**

    - Combat regret through forward momentum. Set achievable goals related to your aspirations. Whether it's developing new skills, expanding your network, or taking calculated risks, action breeds hope and progress.

- **Lead with Curiosity**

  - Life rarely follows our carefully laid plans. Instead of asking, "Will I regret this?" try asking:

    - What exciting possibilities might unfold?
    - What unexpected opportunities could this create?
    - How might this challenge help me grow?

  - This curiosity-driven mindset transforms regret's backward pull into forward momentum. While regret keeps us trapped in past possibilities, curiosity propels us toward future opportunities.

Remember: Regret will always hold you back. Instead of focusing on what you have lost, start concentrating on what you have gained and don't look back.

Reflection Question: Think of a time when regret over a missed or lost opportunity left you feeling stuck. How might you use these tools—reframing, anchoring, or leading with curiosity—to navigate similar situations differently? How can these strategies help you approach future opportunities with greater confidence and openness?

~ LIFE LESSON 7 ~

"You must take the time to understand the horizon within, in order to seek your horizon beyond."

~ Life Lesson 8 ~
Stop Watching - Start Getting Busy: Never Be a Bystander in Life

Within you lies the potential to create meaningful change (which was shared in lesson 6) —a unique combination of experiences, skills, and perspective that only you possess. After years of building your career and gathering life experiences, it's worth asking: What's it all for? Studies consistently show that at life's end, few people wish they had worked longer hours or harder. Instead, many express regret about not having made a greater impact in the world around them.

Breaking the Bystander Effect

It's a common human tendency to notice problems in our communities and assume someone else will address them. This phenomenon, known as the bystander effect, creates a conflicting situation where everyone waits for others to act, and consequently, no one does. Think of a crowded street where someone needs help—the more people present, the less likely any individual is to step forward, each assuming another will take responsibility or has already activated to help the situation.

But what if we flipped this script? What if, instead of waiting for others, we recognized our own capacity to initiate change?

Starting Your Impact Journey

Making a difference doesn't require grand gestures or overwhelming time commitments. It might begin with mentoring someone who could benefit from your experience; volunteering a few hours at a local organization; coaching a community sports team; supporting a neighborhood initiative.

The rewards of engagement extend far beyond the immediate impact. You'll discover new connections, witness tangible improvements in your community, experience a deeper sense of purpose, and find increased personal fulfillment.

Understanding Your Role

People typically fall into three categories when it comes to creating change:

- **Change drivers:** Those actively working to improve their communities and world – these are the few

- **Potential Catalysts:** Those who recognize the need for change but haven't yet found their path forward – these are the many

- **Bystanders:** Those unaware of or disconnected from opportunities for impact – those who are the rest

The 5 A's of Engagement

A more in depth understanding of where you stand and how you can grow, consider this framework:

- **Absent**

    ○ You're unaware of challenges in your community

    ○ Problems seem distant or disconnected from your life

    ○ You haven't considered your potential role in creating change

- **Aware**

    ○ You notice issues around you

    ○ You're beginning to recognize problems but might not fully understand their scope

    ○ You're developing consciousness about community needs

- **Accepting**
    - You understand the challenges
    - You recognize barriers to progress
    - You acknowledge issues but haven't yet taken action

- **Active**
    - You respond when opportunities arise
    - You participate when asked
    - You contribute when structures are in place

- **Advocate**
    - You actively seek opportunities to create change
    - You initiate solutions to community challenges
    - You inspire others to get involved

Considering these 5 A's just listed, where do you see yourself? If you are being honest with yourself and are in the Absent, Aware or Accepting stage, if you want to, how can you move in the Active or Advocate stage?

Moving to Active or Advocate Action

The path to impact begins with a single step. Consider these approaches:

- Connect with friends who are already involved in community work
- Identify local issues that align with your values and reach out to relevant organizations
- Explore your employer's community initiatives and find ways to contribute
- Start small projects that address needs you've noticed in your neighborhood

Remember: The world doesn't need you to solve every problem—it needs you to take action on the ones you can influence. Roll up your sleeves, invite others to join you, and begin making your unique contribution.

Reflection Question: Think about where you fall on the 5 A's of Engagement regarding a specific issue in your community. Whether it's a local concern, a broader societal challenge, or global issue and outline concrete, actionable steps you could take to move from bystander to change-maker. How can you leverage your unique skills and resources to drive meaningful change in this area? Be patient, this will take time.

~ LIFE LESSON 8 ~

"You must leave a lasting impression and not just a footprint."

~ Life Lesson 9 ~
Finding Control in the Uncontrollable with Agency

Life can change in an instant. Whether it's the sudden loss of a job, the death of a loved one, or another profound disruption, these moments can leave us feeling adrift in a storm of emotions. In the immediate aftermath, waves of confusion, grief, and powerlessness can flood our minds, making clear thinking seem impossible. The weight of such experiences can be overwhelming, leaving us feeling like we've lost all control over our lives.

Yet even in our darkest moments, there exists a pathway forward through the power of 'Agency' (a term on how to control the uncontrollable). This isn't just another self-help concept—it's a fundamental shift in how we approach life's challenges. Agency is our ability to acknowledge what has happened while choosing our response rather than letting circumstances dictate our reactions. Without Agency, we're passengers in a runaway vehicle. With it, we reclaim our place in the driver's seat, steering through life's storms with purpose and direction.

~ LIFE LESSON 9 ~

A Personal Journey Through Loss

Let me share a deeply personal story. Within the span of a single year, I lost both my parents. Losing one parent is devastating enough, but losing both in such quick succession was beyond anything I could have imagined. Like anyone would, I experienced profound grief. But then I made a conscious choice to activate my Agency. I refused to let this overwhelming loss define me or pull me into an endless spiral of despair. Instead, I chose to honor their memory by focusing on the beautiful moments we shared and not in what I lost. I faced my grief head-on, challenging it with defiance: "Is this all you've got? I'm still here! You cannot defeat me, and I will not let you." I took control of what was uncontrollable.

Building Agency into Your Life

While everyone's journey through hardship is unique, there are practical ways to develop and strengthen your sense of Agency:

Core foundations

- **Understand your values:** Define the principles that ground you during turbulent times and this bring us back to your anchor points. Having your values becomes your stabilizer and rudder through the difficult times.

- **Recognize your strengths:** Identify and learn to activate your capabilities when facing adversity. Your strengths support your base.

- **Identify triggers:** Become aware of situations or emotions that might compromise your sense of control. Triggers are things that could positively or negatively affect you. Chose the triggers that can overcome the negative emotions and build in the positive experiences.

- **Learn from setbacks:** Transform challenges into opportunities for growth and resilience. Some previous support opportunities have been shared in previous life lessons, see if any of them resonate with you.

Support systems

- **Cultivate positive relationships:** Surround yourself with people who reinforce your sense of Agency.

- **Build professional connections:** Seek mentors and advisors who can guide you through difficult times.

- **Join supportive communities:** Connect with others who share your values and aspirations.

LIFE LESSON 9

Personal practices

- **Embrace mindfulness:** Find your center through meditation, yoga, walking, or other grounding activities. Find something that brings you comfort and supports you through the challenging times.

- **Maintain physical well-being:** Regular exercise and healthy habits strengthen both body and mind. Physical is equally important to the psychological way you may be feeling.

- **Seek professional guidance:** Remember that therapy and counseling can provide valuable perspective and tools. Do not be afraid to reach out as these professionals are there to support you.

Understanding True Agency

It's important to clarify what Agency does and doesn't mean:

Agency Is Not: A superhuman ability to avoid pain or a sign of superiority over others or an emotional detachment from life's challenges.

Agency Is: A conscious choice to take control of your response to life events, an acknowledgment of pain while refusing to be defined by it, a commitment to face challenges with clarity and purpose and the understanding that while we can't control what happens to us, we always control how we respond.

Remember: Building Agency is a journey, not a destination. It's about developing the resilience to face life's challenges while maintaining your sense of self and purpose. In the face of adversity, Agency becomes your anchor, helping you navigate through storms while staying true to your course.

Reflection Question: How do you typically respond to unexpected challenges? Think of a recent difficult situation—how might applying the concept of Agency have changed your response? What steps can you take today to strengthen your sense of Agency for future challenges?

"By walking through the darkness and unknown, I have to rely on my inner light to help guide my way."

~ Life Lesson 10 ~
The Power of Transformation in a Transactional World

Remember our earlier discussion about discovering the 'Extraordinary in the Ordinary'? Let's explore how this principle applies to our daily interactions. Most of us move through life on autopilot, particularly in routine situations. Consider this typical coffee shop exchange:

Barista: "Good morning, how are you?"
You: "Good, how about you?"
Barista: "Good, what can I get you?"
You: "I'll have..."

The interaction ends with a payment, a brief wait, and you continuing your day. It's purely transactional—efficient but mechanical, much like countless exchanges we have in workplaces, schools, and public spaces.

But what if we rewrote this script?

You: "Good morning, how are you?" (you initiate)
Barista: "Good, what can I get you?"

You: "Well, my usual is... but first, what's your favorite drink here?"

This small shift transforms a routine exchange into a moment of genuine connection, often sparking unexpected joy and authentic smiles. By consciously choosing to make someone's day brighter, we elevate mundane moments into meaningful exchanges for both parties. Transformational experiences do not have to be epic and grand. They can be small intentional actions that affect another person in a positive way.

A Lesson in Meaningful Connections

Let me share a transformational story from my time as a university lecturer. After each class, I typically observed two scenarios: most students would rush for the exit, while a few would approach with questions. But one student stood out with her distinctive routine. She would quietly gather her belongings, walk to the door, and patiently wait until I finished addressing other students' questions. Then, with genuine warmth, she would say, "Thank you for today, Professor. Have a great week—see you next time."

During our final class, after her usual thoughtful goodbye, I shared how meaningful her simple gesture had been—how it acknowledged the effort and care invested in each lesson. She seemed surprised, unaware of the lasting impact of her small but intentional action. Years later, her thoughtful interactions remained vivid in my memory, and I have shared her actions in talks and reconnected with her when I visited Korea and we had a lovely dinner and walk together.

~ LIFE LESSON 10 ~

This is the essence of transformational interactions: simple, purposeful actions that create lasting impressions.

The Value of Transformational Exchanges

Why should we prioritize transformation over transaction? These meaningful exchanges:

- Build stronger, more authentic relationships
- Create moments of genuine connection
- Brighten not just others' days, but our own
- Often lead to unexpected opportunities and deeper conversations
- Leave lasting positive impressions on both parties

Creating Transformational Moments

Here's how to elevate your daily interactions from transactional to transformational:

- **Emphasize relationships over results**

    ○ Focus on building meaningful, enduring connections and not superficial networking

    ○ Value the person behind the interaction

    ○ Think long-term rather than seeking immediate benefits

- **Make others feel seen**

  - Acknowledge people's presence and contributions by showing genuine appreciation for their efforts

  - Remember and reference previous conversations

- **Practice active engagement**

  - Give your full, undivided attention

  - Listen with genuine interest

  - Respond thoughtfully to what others share

- **Consider mutual value**

  - Think about what matters to the other person

  - Look for shared interests and common ground

  - Focus on creating value for both parties

- **Choose collaboration over competition**

  - Seek opportunities to work together

  - Share knowledge and resources freely

  - Celebrate collective achievements

~ LIFE LESSON 10 ~

Remember: The beauty of transformational interactions lies in their simplicity. They don't require grand gestures or elaborate plans—just small, mindful adjustments to how we engage with others. These subtle shifts can transform routine encounters into meaningful exchanges that strengthen connections and create lasting positive impacts.

Reflection Question: Think about your routine interactions. Choose one regular exchange in your life—perhaps with a colleague, service worker, or family member. How could you transform this interaction from transactional to transformational? What small change could you make to create a more meaningful connection?

"Don't 'find' the time to meet someone. Instead, 'make' the time.

Finding time means I am busy, and I will try and fit you into my schedule. While making time means that you value the person and need to create time to meet them."

~ Life Lesson 11 ~
Your Big Dreams Start with Small Steps

Two powerful words stand at opposite ends of the spectrum of achievement. One propels us forward toward greatness, while the other subtly works to derail our progress. At first glance, choosing between them might seem obvious, but one often disguises itself as comfort and protection, making its destructive nature harder to recognize.

These two words are 'persistence' and 'limitations.' Persistence drives us forward with unwavering conviction, inspiring us to find paths toward what truly matters. Limitations, however, plant seeds of doubt, whispering reasons why we should abandon our dreams.

The Journey of Achievement

Picture yourself embarking on a meaningful journey. The path ahead seems clear as you take your first steps with determination. But as you progress, limitations begin to surface—perhaps as self-doubt, external criticism, or unexpected obstacles. These voices suggest your goal might be out of reach, tempting you to retreat.

Yet here's the truth: anything truly worth achieving lies within your grasp if you commit to the journey. The real question becomes: Will you persevere despite obstacles, or allow limitations to derail your progress?

A Story of Persistence

Let me share my own story about choosing persistence over limitations. I decided to embark on a journey to reconnect with my ancestral roots in India—a place no one in my family had visited for generations. Armed with only fragments of information and a faded photograph, I began my search, gathering information and building confidence step by step.

The voices of limitation quickly emerged: "You'll never find it," they said. "Why dwell on the past? Focus on the future." Though these doubts echoed around me, I chose not to let them guide my path. Instead, I remained focused on my goal because it was important to me that I discover my past and realize my identity.

The journey wasn't smooth. Moments of discouragement tempted me to give up. But persistence prevailed, and eventually, I found my grandfather's house and discovered relatives we never knew existed. Standing in my ancestral village's fields, I gathered soil to bring back to Canada, gave it to my father, who had never been to our village —a tangible symbol of persistence triumphing over limitations.

Building Persistence and Overcoming Limitations

Here's how to cultivate persistence while navigating past limitations:

- **Set clear objectives**

    ◦ Define specific, measurable, and achievable goals

    ◦ Break large objectives into smaller, manageable tasks

    ◦ Create milestones to track your progress

- **Embrace growth**

    ◦ View challenges as opportunities for learning

    ◦ Replace the word "failure" with "setback"

    ◦ Learn from experiences that don't initially succeed

- **Maintain purpose**

    ◦ Connect with the deeper meaning behind your goals

    ◦ Regularly remind yourself why you started

○ Let your purpose guide you when motivation wavers

- **Develop resilience**

  ○ Accept that setbacks are natural parts of any journey

  ○ Draw strength from past challenges you've overcome

  ○ Build confidence through experience

- **Transform negative self-talk to positive**

  ○ Identify potential mental barriers (noise) that might try to penetrate your decisions

  ○ Reframe any negative thoughts you encounter into empowering statements

  ○ Replace "I can't" with "I'm learning to"

- **Practice consistency**

  ○ Show up regularly, even when progress feels slow, and this might be revisiting your task on a regular basis

  ○ Prioritize steady effort over perfection

  ○ Build momentum through regular action

- **Build support systems**
    - Surround yourself with inspiring individuals
    - Seek mentors who challenge and encourage you to focus on your goal
    - Distance yourself from voices that discourage your dreams

- **Celebrate progress**
    - Acknowledge small victories along the way
    - Recognize each step forward, no matter how minor
    - Use celebrations and small victories to reinforce positive momentum

Remember: Persistence doesn't mean ignoring reality or dismissing genuine challenges. Instead, it means committing to your path with courage, adaptability, and determination. While limitations may attempt to hold you back, persistence will always push you forward—transforming dreams into achievements through a series of small, determined steps.

~ LIFE LESSON 11 ~

Reflection Question: Think about a goal you're currently pursuing. What limitations have you encountered, and how might you use persistence to overcome them? What small steps could you take today to move closer to your objective?

"The voice within must be louder than the noise around you!"

~ Life Lesson 12 ~
Passion to Purpose: What Ignites You?

The common advice to "follow your passion" oversimplifies a complex journey. Passion alone is like a powerful engine without a destination and limited fuel—full of energy but lacking direction. True fulfillment comes from combining passion with purpose, creating a journey that's both energizing and meaningful. The reality though, your purpose may not materialize right away but if you take time and reflect, it may become more accessible.

The Power of Purpose-Driven Passion

Think of passion as your internal spark and purpose as your inner flame. When united, they create an unstoppable force: passion provides the energy to move forward, while purpose ensures you're moving in a meaningful direction. This combination transforms enthusiasm into impact.

While most of us sense there's deeper meaning to our life's journey, uncovering it can seem overwhelming. We've explored tools like anchor points and assessments that can illuminate the path forward, helping make the invisible threads of passion and purpose more tangible. Yet too many of us remain caught in life's daily routines, watching our dreams stay forever on the horizon - close enough to see, but just out of reach.

The tragedy isn't in lacking passion or purpose - it's in allowing the demands of everyday life to drown out their whispers. When we're constantly running on life's treadmill, we rarely pause long enough to hear what truly calls to us. But discovering your passion and purpose isn't a luxury - it's the foundation of a life lived with intention.

Finding Your Path: The Ikigai Framework

The Japanese concept of Ikigai offers a practical approach to discovering where passion meets purpose. It explores four essential questions that can be considered to help discover what really matters to you. Your passion may be within your view but may not allow you to understand your purpose. Consider the four following questions and then see diagram 1:

- What brings you joy? - Identify activities that energize and fulfill you. (your outlet)

- What are your natural talents? - Recognize the unique skills and strengths you bring to the table. (anchor points and assessments)

- How can you create value/make money? - Consider ways to transform your skills into sustainable opportunities. (Realize how to monetize your strengths)

- How can you serve others? - Discover where your abilities meet the world's needs. (What is an opportunity?)

Diagram 1

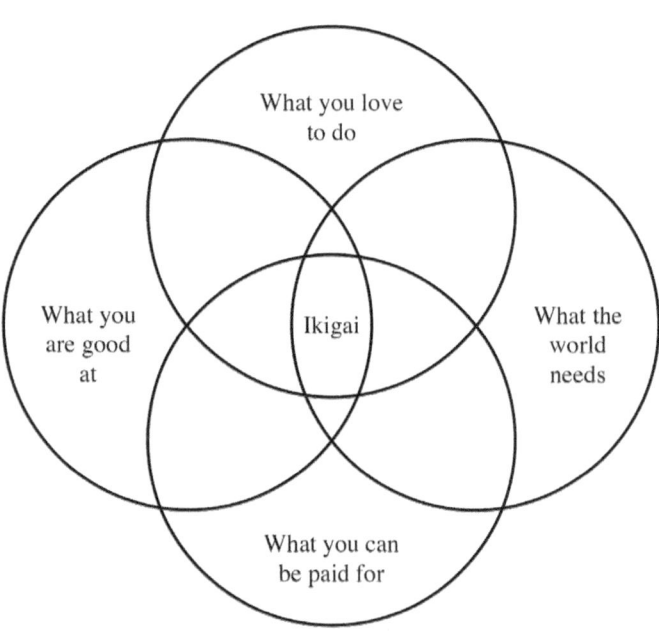

Take a moment: Consider each of the Ikigai sections just listed and reflect on what each means to you and see if you can write some points down to help you realize your Ikigai.

~ LIFE LESSON 12 ~

Transforming Passion into Purposeful Action

- **Discover your spark**

  - Notice what activities make time disappear

  - Identify what topics consistently draw your interest

  - Pay attention to what energizes rather than drains you

- **Connect with meaning**

  - Explore why your passions matter deeply to you

  - Understand how they align with your core values

  - Consider their potential impact on others

- **Create your purpose statement**

  - Craft a clear vision that connects your passion to meaningful impact. For example: "I use my love of technology to make complex systems more accessible to everyone."

- **Build Your Roadmap**

    - Set concrete, achievable goals

    - Break down your vision into actionable steps

    - Start small and build momentum

    - Remain flexible as you grow and evolve

    - Share your journey with key individuals to stay accountable and inspire others

Your purpose isn't just about personal satisfaction—it's about channeling your uniqueness into something larger than yourself, your purpose. By finding this intersection, you create a life that's not only personally rewarding but also meaningful to others.

Remember: Purpose transforms passion from a fleeting spark into a lasting flame. When you align what excites you with what creates meaningful impact, you create a sustainable path to fulfillment and contribution.

Reflection Question: Considering the four zones of Ikigai, take a moment to put your thoughts into each zone and see if it leads you to the start of your Ikigai (purpose) or at least your passion.

~ LIFE LESSON 12 ~

"In order to ignite others, you must first be the flint that strikes your own spark and lights that fire within you."

~ Life Lesson 13 ~
Mind Shift to Supporting Others: Are You a Bucket or a Candle?

"How do you stay so positive?" It's a question I hear often. Reality will dictate that there are challenges and obstacles present, and the answer isn't about avoiding negativity—it's about choosing how we share our energy with the world. This choice comes down to a simple yet powerful question: Are you a bucket or a candle and brings us back to the idea of 'Agency'?

The Bucket vs. The Candle

Imagine two ways of giving energy to others:

As a large bucket, you pour your optimism into others' empty vessels as they approach you with their situation. Each time you give, your resources deplete. Eventually, you run dry, exhausted from constantly giving away pieces of yourself because the bucket does not fill up and just gives.

Instead of a bucket, now think of yourself as a lit candle, you share your flame with others without diminishing your own light. When you ignite others' candles, your flame burns just as bright and is no less depleted. One by one, you illuminate the darkness around you while maintaining your own radiance.

Sustaining Your Light

- **Being a candle requires intentional self-care:**
    - Protect your flame through regular renewal and set clear boundaries to prevent burnout
    - Build emotional resilience by mindfulness practices
    - Connect with others who fuel not drain you
    - Practice gratitude to keep your light burning bright

Your energy isn't a finite resource to be depleted, but a flame to be shared. Let your light shine steadily, illuminating the way for others while keeping your own spark alive.

Remember: You can't light others' paths if your own flame goes out. Like the airplane safety video about when the oxygen mask principle where you put the mask on yourself before helping anyone else —secure your own light first. By viewing yourself as a candle rather than a bucket, you create sustainable positivity that enriches both yourself and others.

Reflection Question: What can you do to feel more like a candle. Provide examples of how you look after yourself.

"Life – To be lived and not solved."

~ Life Lesson 14 ~
As I Wander in Life I Wonder: Explore – Experience – Embrace

Life unfolds as an endless canvas of possibility, inviting us to be travelers rather than tourists on our journey. True wandering isn't aimless—it's a deliberate embrace of discovery that transforms ordinary moments into extraordinary revelations. The path to meaningful flow emerges through three essential channels for us to remember and an easy way to live and reference as the 3Es':

Explore with wonder. Move beyond the familiar, letting curiosity guide you through both your daily life and grander adventures. Every corner of existence—from career to relationships—holds hidden depths waiting to be discovered by those willing to look deeper.

Experience with presence. Don't merely observe life; immerse yourself in its richness. Feel the texture of each moment, engaging fully with both triumphs and challenges. Let every interaction leave its unique imprint on your understanding. Take the time to reflect on what you encounter.

Embrace with intention. Welcome both the expected and unexpected turns in your journey. Each experience, whether joyful or difficult, weaves another thread into your life's tapestry. Through conscious acceptance, even obstacles become opportunities for growth.

This journey isn't to be rushed. Savour it like a fine wine and your journey isn't about reaching a destination—it's about finding meaning in every step. By approaching life as an active explorer rather than a passive observer, you transform simple wandering into purposeful discovery. Your path becomes uniquely yours, shaped by conscious choices and enriched by the wisdom gained along the way.

Remember: Life reveals its deepest treasures not to those who merely pass through, but to those who dare to wonder, wander, and embrace each moment with an open heart.

Reflection Question: Share an example of how you have Explored, Experienced and Embraced. Try to add details and depth to each of the 3E's

"As you travel through life, take your bags with you, but don't forget to fill them with stories and memories."

~ Life Lesson 15 ~
In a World of Critics, Be Someone's Champion

In today's digital age, it's easy to criticize from behind a screen. I learned this firsthand after giving a TEDx talk on personal storytelling. Despite the talk's positive reception, years later someone commented: "Worst TED Talk ever. Stop talking about yourself and reading your notes." The criticism was baseless—I had used just one cue card with three bullet points so I could expand on my thoughts to focus on the audience, and the talk's very purpose was sharing personal stories to help others develop their own.

Instead of responding with anger (which would be a common response), I replied gracefully: "I'm sorry to see this negative comment. While constructive feedback helps me grow, hateful comments often detract from what should be a positive experience. I remain grateful for the opportunity to share my story and help others on their journey."

This experience reinforced a vital truth: we always have a choice in how we show up for others and be presented. Rather than joining the chorus of critics, why not become someone's champion? True championship goes beyond empty praise—it means providing honest guidance, standing beside someone as they grow, and helping them recognize their potential even when they doubt themselves.

When facing negative feedback, remember:

- **Take time before responding.** Your first emotional reaction rarely serves you well. Wait a day, focus on the situation rather than the critic, and respond with grace. In a heated moment, you might be playing into a response they are hoping for and one that does not reflect who you are.

- **Stay grounded in perspective.** One harsh comment doesn't define your worth. Balance it against your achievements and other feedback, though this admittedly takes practice. This is difficult to do because the negative comments do sit with us but remember, that it might just be one person versus the masses.

- **Practice self-care and avoid dwelling.** While it's natural for criticism to sting, don't let it replay endlessly in your mind. Channel that energy into growth instead.

- **Protect your brand.** Don't get pulled into someone else's comments. They are looking for a reaction and if you respond in your own positive way, they are seen as the villain.

To be someone's champion:

- Recognize and believe in their potential, especially when they struggle to see it themselves

- Offer honest, constructive feedback that helps them grow

- Create a safe space for them to share fears and aspirations without judgment

- Celebrate their victories without taking credit

- Share resources and opportunities that align with their goals

- Show up consistently, in both challenges and triumphs

- Lead by example and inspire through your actions

- Practice patience, knowing that growth takes time

In a world quick to tear down, choose to build up. Be the person who helps others shine. This choice creates ripples of positivity that extend far beyond any single interaction, fostering an environment where mutual success and growth can flourish, and your personal brand is one that people will appreciate.

Remember: Every person needs someone in their corner. Why not be that someone? You never know how much of a positive influence you can be on someone's journey through life.

Reflection Question: Share an example of a time you had helped someone and what was that experience like and how did it make you feel?

"You might be the key that unlocks someone's future."

~ Life Lesson 16 ~
Managing Others' Commitments: Clear Boundaries for Better Balance

The request for help by others often puts us in a challenging situation: say yes and risk overextending yourself and putting your own priorities at risk or say no and potentially damage relationships and be seen as someone who does not contribute. But this apparent dilemma overlooks a powerful third option: "Here's what I can do."

This approach transforms a binary choice of yes or no into a collaborative discussion. Instead of choosing between total commitment and complete refusal, you create space for meaningful contribution on your own terms. I experienced this firsthand when a nonprofit invited me to join their board. Rather than declining outright, I offered to serve as an advisor, providing targeted guidance while maintaining sustainable boundaries.

Even in situations with less flexibility, like workplace assignments, you can still navigate requests strategically. Instead of a simple yes or no, discuss workload balance, timeline adjustments, or potential resource needs with your supervisor.

When managing commitments, consider these principles:

- Understand the context - Evaluate the request's importance and urgency. Consider both the asking party's needs and your existing commitments. This understanding helps you propose realistic alternatives that serve everyone's interests.

- Communicate thoughtfully - Address situations early and honestly, but diplomatically. Explain your constraints while showing genuine interest in supporting their goals. This maintains trust even when you can't fulfill the original request.

- Offer alternatives - Focus on what you can contribute rather than what you can't do. Perhaps you can provide limited assistance, connect them with other resources, or help later. Frame your response in terms of possibilities rather than limitations.

- Preserve relationships - End the conversations positively, keeping doors open for future collaboration. A thoughtful "no" today, coupled with genuine support within your means, often leads to better opportunities tomorrow.

~ LIFE LESSON 16 ~

Remember: Setting boundaries isn't about refusing help—it's about ensuring you can contribute meaningfully and sustainably. By clearly communicating what you can do, you maintain both your effectiveness and your relationships, creating better outcomes for everyone involved.

Reflection Question: Think about a response you can try to use the next time where you are confronted with a situation where you are asked to take on a responsibility.

"Good intentions are as helpful as a leaky bucket...eventually, they will both be empty. What ever you promise, be sure to over deliver because your reputation is on the line."

~ Life Lesson 17 ~
*Intentions vs. Goals:
A Path to Authentic Living*

We live in a goal-obsessed world. From childhood, we're asked about our life ambitions and career objectives, pressured to map out our future in precise detail and if not well thought out, may not even focus on our passions or purpose. While this traditional approach to achievement isn't inherently flawed, there's a more fluid and potentially more fulfilling alternative: living with intention. It is not wrong to have goals but rather, intentions become a different way to map out your path.

Goals, by nature, offer a rigid destination. They create a binary world of success or failure, forcing us to commit to specific outcomes in an unpredictable future. When life presents unexpected opportunities or the environment shifts before us, we face an unnecessary dilemma: stick to our predetermined path or venture into promising unknown territory. Simply put - do I give up the goal or the opportunity?

Intentions, however, operate differently. Rather than fixing our sights on distant targets, they guide us through anchor points—our core values and non-negotiable priorities that define who we are. As mentioned at the outset, these anchor points serve as a compass rather than a map, allowing us to evaluate opportunities based on alignment with our deeper purpose. If goals are important to you, this is not to say you are wrong but rather to provide you an alternative that might make more sense.

My own journey illustrates this distinction. I never set a goal to become an author, but when the opportunity arose, it resonated perfectly with my anchor points. This alignment provided the clarity to embrace this unexpected path without hesitation.

Living with Intention: Listed are practical tips to allow you to shift from goals to intensions if the concept aligns with you.

- **Define your anchor points** – Reflect on the words you have chosen and what truly matters to you: your core values, sources of joy, and fundamental beliefs. These become your decision-making framework.

- **Transform goals into intentions** - Rather than declaring "I will lose 10 pounds in 4 months," shift to "I will cultivate healthier habits and focus on my physical and mental health in the following ways…." This subtle change focuses on the journey rather than just the destination.

- **Embrace the process** - While goals fixate on endpoints, intentions celebrate the entire journey. They encourage presence and gratitude for each step, creating fulfillment beyond mere achievement.

- **Maintain flexible purpose** - Intentions allow you to pivot while staying true to your values. When opportunities arise, evaluate them against your anchor points rather than predetermined goals.

Remember: Life rarely follows a straight line. By choosing intentions over rigid goals, you create space for unexpected opportunities while remaining true to your authentic self. This approach doesn't mean abandoning ambition—it means pursuing it with greater wisdom, flexibility, and personal truth.

Your path forward isn't about checking boxes; it's about creating a life that resonates with who you truly are.

Reflection Question: Are you more comfortable with goals or intentions and express why.

"When I was younger, I sought stability and comfort because it was safe. Now that I am older, I look back and wonder if all the stability and comfort prevented me from enjoying what life had to give."

~ Life Lesson 18 ~
Change Your Words – Change Your World

Words carry weight far beyond their dictionary definitions. I witnessed this firsthand when a student visited my office, repeatedly emphasizing "problems" in our conversation. When I asked about solutions, his silence spoke volumes—he had become so focused on obstacles that possibilities and opportunities had faded from view.

The language we choose shapes both our reality and others' perceptions of us. Someone who consistently highlights problems may unintentionally build a reputation as a complainer, while one who speaks of opportunities tends to be seen as a problem-solver.

Consider the word "failure." It's often treated as a necessary step toward success, but true failure only occurs when we completely surrender. What most call failure is a setback—a temporary pause in progress, not a permanent end. Think of a situation that did not work, as a setback where we get back up, dust ourselves off, learn from the experience, and emerge stronger. This subtle shift in terminology can transform our response to challenges: instead of accepting defeat, we recognize an opportunity for growth.

Transforming Our Chosen Words from Challenges to Opportunities – see the list of examples:

- Problems → Frame them as opportunities for growth

- Weaknesses → View them as areas for development

- Mistakes → Embrace them as learning moments

- Conflicts → Recognize them as differences in perspective

- Criticism → Welcome it as constructive feedback

- Obstacles → Approach them as hurdles to overcome

- Rejection → See it as guidance toward alternative paths

- Uncertainty → Appreciate it as an invitation to flexibility

- Limitations → Treat them as boundaries to explore

The shift extends beyond simple word substitution. When we say, "fully engaged" instead of "overwhelmed," or "progress not yet realized" rather than "failure to achieve," we're not just choosing gentler terms—we're adopting a more empowering perspective. What this involves is not just saying the words but being conscious and understanding of the impact the words hold. You might start catching yourself with your words and then try framing them with a better objective and purpose.

This mindful approach to language isn't about denying challenges or sugar-coating difficulties. Instead, it's about framing situations in ways that emphasize possibility over limitation, growth over stagnation, and progress over perfection.

Remember: Your words don't just describe your world—they create it. Choose them wisely and watch how your reality transforms in response.

Reflection Question: Are there any words you can think of that you use a lot and maybe consider a replacement word or words that allows a more positive frame of mind?

"Society says we should make a weakness into a strength. Unfortunately, you will waste a lot of time and effort, and it will likely never be a strength.

Instead, focus on your strength and bring your weakness to an acceptable level."

~ Life Lesson 19 ~
Perceptions: Are they Truths or Just Our Own Personal Truths

Every person views the world through a unique lens, shaped by their experiences, relationships, education, and countless other influences. These individual perspectives aren't universal truths—they're personal truths that colour how we interpret and interact with the world around us.

Consider a simple exercise I use in corporate workshops: I show participants an image of the ocean and ask for one-word descriptions. The responses paint a fascinating spectrum: "serene," "dangerous," "blue," "waves," "beautiful," "treacherous," even unexpected words like "sushi," "mermaids," or "pirates." I ask the group, which is the correct word. They will respond with various words, such as water, but I say that they are not correct. Confused, the audience asks me what the correct word is. Then I declare that only one word—"calm"—is correct and they look confused because they may not agree.

This typically sparks protest. I push further, suggesting that those who said "calm" or "serene" would make ideal team members for me because they align to calm, while those who saw danger or offered creative alternatives might not fit because they are not on the same page as me. Just as the disagreement peaks, I pose a crucial question: "Why would I need someone who sees danger whereas I and others see calm?

The answer reveals itself through discussion: Those who spot potential dangers bring valuable risk awareness. Those who see "pirates" or "mermaids" offer a finer detail perspective that others might miss. Each unique viewpoint contributes to a more complete understanding of the whole and benefits the team.

To Embrace Different Perspectives:

- **Listen actively** - Focus fully on understanding others' viewpoints before formulating your response. Practice repeating their ideas to ensure genuine comprehension.

- **Approach with curiosity** - Ask open-ended questions that invite deeper explanation. Your goal isn't to agree or disagree, but to understand the journey that led to their perspective.

- **Seek diversity** - Deliberately engage with people whose backgrounds and experiences differ from yours. Each unique viewpoint adds depth to your understanding.

- **Suspend judgment -** Enter conversations with an open mind, recognizing that your personal truth isn't the only truth. Remember: when emotions rise, logic often falls.

Remember: True strength lies not in defending our perspective but in embracing and respecting the viewpoints around us. By welcoming diverse perspectives, we don't just solve problems more effectively—we enrich our understanding of the world itself. This isn't about finding a single "right" answer. It's about recognizing that each perspective, like a different facet of a gemstone, reveals something valuable about the whole.

Reflection Question: Think about where your own perspectives emerge from and think about how you might be able to expand your thoughts by realizing that they are your truths, but others may have a different perspective.

"Myth – Theory – Practice
A myth is a story of what we
think the world should be.
Theory is the logical explanation
but not proven. Practice is the
application and if it works."

~ Life Lesson 20 ~
The 15-70-15 Rule: Don't Take It Personally

When giving a presentation, have you ever noticed how your attention gravitates toward that one person checking their phone or looking disinterested, even while others are actively engaged? This common experience can leave even seasoned speakers feeling discouraged.

During my years as a university lecturer, I encountered this regularly. In lecture halls filled with 100 students, I'd inevitably spot a few scrolling through their phones or staring at laptops, leaving me uncertain about their engagement. This observation often led me to question my teaching effectiveness.

The breakthrough came when I developed the '15-70-15 Rule', which breaks down typical audience engagement into three segments:

The 15-70-15 Distribution:

- **Bottom 15%:** These individuals either strongly dislike your presentation or show no interest

- **Middle 70%:** This majority ranges from finding moderate value to being quite engaged but seeking more
- **Top 15%:** These are your enthusiastic supporters who find exceptional value in your message

This framework revealed an important insight: the bottom 15% will likely remain disengaged regardless of your efforts, while the top 15% are already committed and you don't need to worry about them. The key is focusing your energy on the middle 70%, where you have the greatest opportunity to increase engagement.

Maximize Your Impact:

- Maintain your focus on the partially engaged majority. While it's tempting to fixate on disinterested participants, this only diverts energy from those who are actively participating.

- Remain authentic in your delivery. Your natural style will resonate with most of your audience, even if it doesn't connect with everyone.

- Gather feedback strategically. While it's valuable to understand why some participants disengage, avoid making sweeping changes that might alienate your supportive majority who might flip to the less engaged.

- Demonstrate genuine interest in all participants. Even when facing disengagement, showing you

~ LIFE LESSON 20 ~

care about everyone's experience can sometimes bridge the gap.

- Maintain your perspective and development. Remember that universal appeal is rarely achievable, and that's perfectly acceptable. Focus instead on continuous improvement for the benefit of your engaged audience.

Remember: By embracing the 15-70-15 Rule, you can shift your focus from those few disengaged individuals to the larger group who appreciate your message. This perspective allows you to celebrate your successes while maintaining realistic expectations about audience engagement.

Reflection Question: Think of a time where you can apply the rule of 15-70-15 and consider how you reacted and if it was not as positive as you would have hoped, what could you do to improve your situation?

"I may not be able to change the world, people or circumstances. What I can do is alter my attitude and face what is given. I will try and see things from a more accepting lens and not take things personally."

~ Life Lesson 21 ~
Leadership Beyond the Title: A Life-Driven Approach

When someone tells me they want to be a leader, I often ask them to pause and consider what that really means. Many pursue leadership through countless books, workshops, and training programs, searching for that perfect formula to earn the title or to have an impressive title on their door. But here's what most miss: authentic leadership isn't about claiming a title—it's about earning trust. It goes back to a much earlier life lesson about understanding 'who' you are and not 'what' you do.

Let me share a conversation I frequently have:

"I want to be a leader," someone will tell me.
"Why did you come to me?" I ask.
"Because you're a leader," they respond.
"What makes me a leader?" and I get many responses and beautiful words but none of them are correct.

Their answers typically focus on traits like integrity, caring or communication skills. But I always challenge this perspective:

"Those qualities are great and valuable, but they don't make me a leader. Only one thing does." Now this person is about to receive the one thing that makes them a leader and they lean in with anticipation. I share with them that the one thing that makes me a leader are 'followers,' the people around me who decide if I have earned their trust. Leadership exists because people choose to follow—not because someone holds a position.

This response often startles people. Some immediately ask how to gain more followers, but that's missing the point. The real question is: Are you worthy of being followed? Leadership isn't self-declared—it's recognized by others through your actions, decisions, and character. I like to always say that leadership is not a place, position or title, leadership is a lifestyle, and you don't determine if you are a leader, those around you will say if you are worthy of the title.

Leadership as a Way of Life

Think of leadership like the sword referenced in Sun Tzu's ancient wisdom: "A gentleman keeps a sword by his side." Leadership, like that sword, should be ready when needed but doesn't need constant display. It's not about maintaining an authoritative presence 24/7—it's about knowing when to step forward and when to step back. When to take the sword out and when to put it away.

Core Elements of Authentic Leadership

To cultivate genuine leadership qualities, focus on developing these fundamental attributes:

- Your personality should balance approachability with reliability. Be visible and engaging. Your actions speak volumes so make sure there is alignment between what you say and what you do.

- Develop a strong self-concept—know your values and stand firmly by them. Your confidence should stem from this clear sense of identity. The anchor points can be of significant help here.

- Let your motivation come from a genuine desire to guide and support others. When your enthusiasm for supporting your team is authentic, it naturally creates purposeful direction. Be transformational over transactional by showing you care about their well-being.

- Maintain moderate drive instead of overdrive —push for achievement while remaining mindful not to overwhelm your team. Success should unite, not divide. It is about balancing the process and the people.

~ LIFE LESSON 21 ~

- Make integrity your foundation. When your actions consistently align with your stated values, trust naturally follows.

- Get proficient in your work and develop a deep understanding of your field. Your expertise breeds confidence, both in yourself and from your team.

- Cultivate both knowledge and practical intelligence. Learn to process complex information while maintaining the ability to delegate effectively and make clear decisions.

- Develop your emotional intelligence. Your capacity to understand and manage both your emotions and those around you. This creates an environment where everyone can thrive because each person is respected.

- The essence of leadership isn't in pursuing the role—it's in becoming someone others choose to follow. Focus on embodying these qualities authentically, and leadership will emerge naturally from the trust and respect you earn.

Remember: Simply put, true leadership is bestowed by others, not claimed by oneself so stop chasing the title.

Reflection Question: Examine your background and focus on how you might embrace this perspective of leadership where you allow others to determine that you are a leader. Are you comfortable with this concept?

"Leadership is not a place, position or a title. Leadership is a lifestyle. The basic truth is that you don't determine if you are a leader... the people around you determine if you are worthy of the title."

~ Life Lesson 22 ~
A Universal Truth: The More You Share, the More You Gain

Everyone collects unique experiences and insights throughout their life's journey. The question is: what will you do with this accumulated wisdom? While it's natural to hold onto our hard-earned knowledge for fear of others stealing our worth, there's profound value in sharing it with others—though not indiscriminately.

Many hesitate to share, feeling they haven't achieved enough to offer valuable guidance. But consider this: if a new colleague joined your workplace tomorrow, wouldn't you be able to help them navigate their first days? This simple reality proves you have something worthwhile to contribute.

Of course, concerns about being taken advantage of are valid. Sharing isn't about giving everything to everyone—it's about thoughtfully offering your insights to those who genuinely value them. While success is often measured in financial terms and status, there's another crucial dimension: personal fulfillment. When you share your expertise authentically, you often discover that fulfillment attracts success naturally. People are drawn to those who find genuine satisfaction in helping others grow. Think of it this way: people chase money and status but rather than chasing, if you start building fulfillment, money and status will come to you.

The key lies in authenticity. Share because you want to help, not because you expect immediate returns. Think of it like pushing a cart uphill until your consistent efforts build momentum, and the natural flow of reciprocity takes over.

Meaningful Ways to Share Your Journey:

- **Through mentorship** - You can guide others while honing your own leadership skills. The satisfaction of seeing others succeed often leads to unexpected opportunities and deeper professional relationships.

- **Public speaking** – You might not be comfortable sharing at the outset, but getting relaxed as a speaker takes time, will boost your confidence and helps establish you as a thought leader. Start with topics you know well, and don't hesitate to collaborate. Your confidence will grow with practice, while your network expands through meaningful connections.

- **Build relationships** - One-on-one conversations and event participation creates memorable connections. These authentic interactions often lead to natural referrals and partnerships.

~ LIFE LESSON 22 ~

- **Volunteering your expertise** – Seek out organizations aligned with your values builds community trust while connecting you with like-minded individuals who may become future collaborators.

- **Project collaboration** – Seek out opportunities outside your primary role which broadens your skill set while fostering innovation. These experiences often lead to unexpected professional growth opportunities.

Remember: sharing your experiences isn't about depleting your resources—it's about creating ripples of positive impact that often return in unexpected ways. This goes back to a previous life lesson about changing the world through your actions.

Reflection Question: How might be a simple way you could share your experiences with others? Could it be through a formal mentorship process or perhaps an informal conversation?

"Universal truth - Compete against others, no one wins. Compete against myself, everyone wins!"

~ Life Lesson 23 ~
The Beauty of Imperfection: Understanding Wabi-Sabi

In our relentless pursuit of perfection, we often miss an essential truth: perfection itself can be a flaw. While society pushes us toward flawlessness, this chase can become an exhausting cycle of constant refinement, leaving us drained and further from our objectives as we dedicate a lot of time to fix something to a level of perfection.

Enter Wabi-sabi, the Japanese philosophy that finds beauty in imperfection. This concept challenges our conventional understanding of beauty and worth, suggesting that flaws aren't defects to be corrected but rather characteristics that give objects—and people—their unique essence.

I discovered the power of this philosophy unexpectedly while shopping online. A brass Buddha statue caught my attention, listed as "flawed" due to brass firing that left an uneven base, and surface blemishes. Rather than deterring me, these imperfections drew me in. When it arrived, I found myself cherishing these supposed flaws—they made the piece uniquely mine, reflecting the

~ LIFE LESSON 23 ~

beautiful imperfection we all carry within ourselves...my own flaws. Some may purely buy this Buddha because it was on sale, but few would buy it just because it had imperfections.

This experience highlighted a crucial distinction between perfection and quality. Perfection demands endless tweaking, often at the cost of progress and peace of mind. It can strain relationships and amplify our insecurities. Quality, however, focuses on creating something meaningful and worthwhile without the burden of absolute flawlessness.

Consider this perspective: while perfection demands 100%, quality thrives at a respectable 90%. At this level, your work maintains excellence while remaining adaptable and grounded. You don't need to announce that you're intentionally stopping short of perfection—simply move forward knowing you've created something valuable.

Release yourself from the burden of perfection. Find beauty in the knots, curves, and blemishes that make something uniquely authentic. Wabi-sabi reminds us that true beauty lies not in flawlessness, but in discovering the extraordinary within the seemingly imperfect.

Remember: Embracing Wabi-sabi liberates us from the exhausting pursuit of perfection. It teaches us that imperfections aren't flaws to be fixed but rather elements that add character and depth to our work and lives. Quality isn't about settling—it's about recognizing that genuine effort and authenticity matter more than flawless execution.

Reflection Question: What are your thoughts on Wabi Sabi and are you able to pinpoint any imperfections you hold? If you can find an imperfection you have, how might you embrace it and not focus on it as a negative?

"To be perfect is an imperfection. Look in the mirror and really examine who you are. We can focus on our flaws as a weakness, but they may be our unique differentiator masking our magnificence."

~ Life Lesson 24 ~
Appreciative Inquiry: Unlocking Personal Growth Through Strengths

While our instinct often drives us to focus on fixing problems, there's a more powerful approach to personal development. Rather than addressing deficiencies, what if we built upon our existing strengths? This is where 'Appreciative Inquiry,' traditionally a business change tool, offers valuable insights for individual growth.

At its core, Appreciative Inquiry shifts our perspective from "What needs fixing?" to "What's already working well, and how can we amplify it?" This fundamental change in mindset transforms personal development from a process of correction to one of enhancement.

Let's explore the four phases of Appreciative Inquiry—known as the 4 D's, and their focus on personal growth:

- **Discovery:** Uncovering what your strengths are not deficiencies – The identify phase

    ○ Begin by identifying what's already working well in your life. Reflect on your moments of triumph, peak experiences, and natural talents. This isn't just about listing achievements—it's about understanding the unique qualities that led to your successes. What skills came naturally? When did you feel most energized and effective?

- **Dream:** Envisioning your ideal future – The vision phase

  - Building on your discovered strengths, imagine your ideal future. This isn't about realistic limitations—it's about possibility. What impact do you want to make? What kind of work makes you come alive? Your dream should align with your authentic strengths while stretching your vision of what's possible.

- **Design:** Generate your path forward – The create phase

  - With your strengths identified and future envisioned, develop concrete strategies to bridge the gap. This phase involves creating actionable plans that leverage your existing capabilities while developing new ones. Consider what skills you need to acquire, relationships to build, and opportunities to pursue.

~ LIFE LESSON 24 ~

- **Delivery:** Making it happen – The action phase

    ○ The final phase focuses on implementation and sustainability. Take deliberate steps toward your vision while maintaining flexibility. Celebrate progress, adjust course when needed, and keep building on your strengths. Remember that setbacks aren't failures—they're opportunities to apply your strengths in new ways.

Remember: By embracing Appreciative Inquiry, you transform personal development from a process of fixing weaknesses into a journey of amplifying strengths. This positive approach not only leads to more sustainable growth but also creates greater fulfillment along the way.

Reflection Question: Instead of a problem or challenge, focus on something you hold that is a strength and apply it to each of the 4D approach.

"Can you be good at something you don't believe in? Sure, but you will never be great at it."

~ Life Lesson 25 ~
The Truth Behind Imposter Syndrome: You Are Enough

We all know that gnawing fear of feeling inadequate—of believing we're not qualified enough despite evidence to the contrary. This is imposter syndrome: the persistent voice questioning our worth, whispering "You're not ready" even as others recognize our potential.

Picture receiving a promotion you've earned through years of dedicated work. Instead of celebrating, you're paralyzed by doubt: "Am I truly qualified? What if I fail spectacularly?" These thoughts can overshadow years of experience, making our accomplishments feel insignificant against the mountain of perceived inadequacies.

Remember this truth: You were born with wings. This isn't just a metaphor—it represents the innate capabilities, experiences, and support system you've built throughout your years. These wings have been strengthened by every challenge you've overcome and every triumph you've achieved as well as people around you who won't let you fall.

~ LIFE LESSON 25 ~

Conquering imposter syndrome isn't about reckless leaps into the unknown. It's about recognizing the strength of your wings and using them wisely.

Here's how to soar above self-doubt:

- Acknowledge the feeling. Imposter syndrome is a common experience, not a reflection of your capabilities. Learn to recognize these thoughts for what they are—temporary doubts, not permanent truths.

- Challenge your inner critic with evidence of your accomplishments. Keep an ongoing record of your achievements, skills, and milestones. This isn't about ego—it's about maintaining perspective when doubt creeps in.

- Build your support network. Connect with mentors, colleagues, and friends who believe in you. Their perspective can help ground you when your confidence wavers.

- Stop measuring yourself against others. Focus on your unique journey and growth instead of comparing your chapter one to someone else's chapter twenty.

- Embrace continuous learning. Not knowing everything isn't a weakness—it's an opportunity for growth. Fill knowledge gaps through education, mentorship, and practical experience.

- Practice self-compassion. Treat yourself with the same kindness you'd offer a friend facing similar doubts. Acknowledge your efforts and progress, not just your perceived shortcomings.

- Set realistic standards. Remember the wisdom of wabi-sabi—perfection isn't the goal. Focus on quality and continuous improvement instead.

- Seek constructive feedback from trusted sources. Use this input to grow and develop, not as ammunition for self-doubt.

- Celebrate your unique contributions. Your distinctive perspective and abilities bring value that others might not possess.

Remember: Imposter syndrome is a mindset, not a life sentence. With patience and intentional effort, you can overcome these doubts and flourish. Your wings are stronger than you realize—trust them to carry you forward.

Reflection Question: Have you ever encountered imposter syndrome where you felt you were not good enough? What did that feel like? Do your anchor points help establish a base of more confidence?

~ LIFE LESSON 25 ~

"When you stop using words like won't, can't or shouldn't, then you can unlock your possibilities."

~ Life Lesson 26 ~
Navigating Your Journey: Past, Present, and Future

Life moves continuously, often in directions we don't fully comprehend. But imagine shaping that journey with greater purpose through a saying: "To envision your future, you must reflect on your past while standing firmly in the present." This perspective illuminates how balancing all three dimensions of time can create a more meaningful path forward.

Understanding Your Past

Your history holds a treasury of experiences and insights. Like a well-worn map, it shows the terrain you've crossed—your triumphs, challenges, and pivotal moments. It provides the foundation of your anchor points. While these experiences shouldn't bind you to what was, they provide invaluable tools for navigating what lies ahead. Your past isn't a destination to dwell in, but rather a collection of lessons that strengthen your journey forward.

- LIFE LESSON 26 -

Embracing the Present

The present moment offers a unique vantage point—a place to pause, reflect, and chart your course. Too often, we rush through our days, caught in routines without truly appreciating where we stand. This moment is your platform for evaluation, where you can align your past experiences with future aspirations. It's here that you can clearly see both where you've been and where you might go.

Shaping Your Future

When you combine insights from your past with present awareness, the future becomes less daunting. Instead of stepping blindly forward, you move with purpose and confidence. Your experiences provide stability, while your present consciousness ensures thoughtful direction. The horizon ahead transforms from an uncertain void into an exciting landscape of possibilities.

How to Weave the Three Dimensions Together:

- Examine your defining moments—those milestones and challenges that shaped your values and perspectives. Look for patterns in these experiences that reveal what truly energizes you.

- Document your journey through regular journaling. Even a few minutes daily can capture valuable insights that illuminate your path forward.

- Celebrate your achievements, no matter their size. Understanding what led to past successes helps build confidence for future challenges.

- Learn from setbacks without dwelling on them. Extract the wisdom from difficult experiences to guide future decisions.

- Reflect on meaningful relationships—both positive and challenging ones. Consider what kind of support system you need to thrive moving forward.

- Revisit abandoned dreams and goals. Are they still relevant? Have they evolved into new aspirations?

- Seek perspectives from trusted mentors and friends but maintain your own focus. Others' insights can illuminate blind spots without dictating your direction but be cautious of their biases.

- Envision your desired legacy. Let your core values and strengths serve as anchor points guiding you toward meaningful impact.

Remember: A fulfilling journey doesn't emerge from focusing solely on the future or dwelling in the past. It comes from weaving together all three dimensions of time—honoring your history, engaging fully with the present, and moving purposefully toward tomorrow. This integration creates a life story that's uniquely yours, rich with meaning and intentional growth.

~ LIFE LESSON 26 ~

Reflection Question: Consider your current life and select one aspect (work, family life, or school) and then examine how the past has gotten you here and maybe where the future will go based on past and present.

"To vision the future, reflect on the past while standing in the present."

~ Life Lesson 27 ~
Winning the Lottery but Losing the Ticket

Imagine discovering you hold a winning lottery ticket. Now consider this: you're surrounded by potential winning tickets every day. These aren't paper slips from the corner store—they're the meaningful connections you make with others, each one potentially life-changing.

Let me share a revealing encounter. I once met a well-dressed young man downtown, studying papers with a look of confusion. When I offered help, he explained he was searching for a hotel to submit his hotel management resume. Since I was heading to the hotel next door, I offered to walk with him. During our conversation, learning about his hotel management diploma and career aspirations, I offered to connect him with my contacts at several prestigious hotels and I handed him my business card, anticipating an email that never came.

This story illustrates a profound truth about opportunity: it often appears in unexpected moments. Whether he lost the card, doubted the sincerity of the offer, or found another path, a potential door remained unopened. In my experience, only about one in twenty people follow through on such opportunities—and it's these individuals, who do reach out, often find themselves benefiting from unexpected support and connections.

Here's how to recognize and capitalize on these hidden opportunities:

- Approach each interaction with intention. Treat every meaningful encounter as a potential stepping stone to something greater.

- Focus on building genuine connections rather than collecting contacts. Quality relationships exceed quantity every time.

- Create mutual value. Look for ways to contribute to others' success while remaining open to how they might enrich your journey.

- Stay curious and open-minded. Meaningful connections often emerge from unexpected conversations.

- Maintain professionalism and positivity in all interactions. You never know who you might be speaking with.

- Expand your connections thoughtfully. Each conversation potentially links you to an entire web of valuable relationships and opportunities.

- Most crucially, follow up. This simple step often separates those who merely encounter opportunities from those who seize them.

- Remain prepared for opportunity without forcing outcomes. The most valuable connections often develop organically when we stay open to possibilities and while building those authentic relationships with those we encounter.

Remember: Every interaction carries potential—like a lottery ticket waiting to be claimed. By nurturing meaningful relationships and staying intentional in your connections, you create a life rich with opportunities for growth and fulfillment. The winning tickets are already in your hands; the question is, will you cash them in?

Reflection Question: Think back to a time where you had a potential winning lottery ticket. Is there someone you have not talked to in a while? Why not just drop them a note and tell them you were thinking about them.

~ LIFE LESSON 27 ~

"Who was there to support me, and I let them slip away? Who cared about my future, and I did not follow up?

Who was to blame in this... me? It is never too late to reignite a connection."

~ Life Lesson 28 ~
Beyond Earning a Living: How to Truly Live

Have you found yourself caught in life's routine—where days blur together in an endless cycle of work and obligations? When money becomes your primary motivator, it's easy to lose touch with the passion and energy that once drove you. Take a moment to consider: Are you merely earning a living, or are you truly living which incorporates your purpose.

While earning an income is necessary, it shouldn't define your entire existence. True living encompasses both financial stability and personal fulfillment. When money becomes our sole focus, it often ends up controlling our lives rather than supporting them.

The journey to a more fulfilling life begins with acknowledging your desire for something beyond the everyday. Here's how to infuse your life with greater meaning and vitality:

- **Embrace spontaneity and transform your daily activities.** Break free from routine by saying "yes" to unexpected opportunities. Try new restaurants or explore unfamiliar places. Small adventures can bring you fresh perspective.

- **Pursue long-held interests.** Whether it's learning an instrument, taking up painting, or joining a sports league—it's never too late to start something new. Find activities that spark joy and engagement.

- **Set meaningful SMART goals in what ever you chose:**

    - Specific: Define clear objectives

    - Measurable: Track your progress

    - Achievable: Ensure it's within reach

    - Relevant: Align with your values

    - Time-bound: Set clear deadlines

- **Value experiences over possessions.** While material things offer temporary satisfaction, meaningful experiences create lasting memories. Travel, attend concerts, or spend quality time with loved ones.

- **Practice mindfulness.** Take time to appreciate life's simple pleasures—a stunning sunset, moving music, or quiet moments of reflection. Slow down and savor the present moment.

- **Rebalance your life.** Evaluate how you spend your time between work and social activities. Ensure you're giving enough attention to what truly matters. Ensure you have an outlet that provides you mental space (see lesson 29).

- **Engage your community.** Volunteer, join local groups, or simply be a tourist in your own town. Fresh perspectives often come from connecting with others and exploring your surroundings.

- **Nurture meaningful relationships.** Spend time with people who uplift and inspire you. These connections create lasting memories and provide essential support. Remember the life lesson on being a candle and not a bucket, these people keep that flame lit.

- **Keep learning.** Challenge yourself with new skills or knowledge. Whether through formal courses or casual exploration, continuous learning adds richness to life.

- **Practice gratitude.** End each day by noting three things you're thankful for—not just major events, but simple moments that brought joy. This practice helps shift focus from what's missing to what's present.

~ LIFE LESSON 28 ~

Remember: Life isn't meant to be merely survived—it's meant to be lived fully and authentically. By making intentional changes and embracing opportunities for growth, you can create a life that feels vibrant and truly your own.

Reflection Question: Consider the last point about practicing gratitude. What are you grateful for? Why does what you selected matter to you?

"Are you just earning a living or are you really living?"

~ Life Lesson 29 ~
The Essential Outlet: How to Reconnect and Recharge

Life extends far beyond your profession. While work is one piece of who you are, it shouldn't define your entire existence. Yet often, as it has been shared, we become so consumed by daily demands that time blurs—days blend into months, months into years, until we find ourselves wondering what we've truly accomplished. In this constant rush, how are we nurturing ourselves?

Enter the concept of an outlet—an activity beyond work that infuses joy into your life. This might be tending a garden, losing yourself in books, taking mindful walks, experimenting in the kitchen, or spending quality time with loved ones. The key is identifying what brings you genuine joy and making it a consistent part of your life.

Consider this question: "How can I build a house if I continue to put out my daily fires?" When we're constantly reacting to life's demands without taking time to reset, how can we tackle the meaningful challenges before us? An outlet creates the mental space needed to approach complex problems with fresh perspective. An outlet is not something difficult but rather something to be enjoyed.

Here's why having an outlet is crucial for holistic well-being:

- **Stress relief:** Without healthy ways to decompress from life's pressures, you risk burnout, anxiety, and various health complications.

- **Emotional expression:** Your outlet provides a safe space to process and express emotions—a vital aspect of mental health, not a sign of weakness.

- **Creative growth:** Dedicating time to an outlet often unlocks unexpected creative potential. Sometimes, these pursuits even evolve into meaningful ventures or businesses.

- **Mental clarity:** A busy mind struggles to focus on life's important details. Regular engagement with your outlet helps clear mental fog and offers new perspectives.

- **Physical vitality:** Medical research shows that prolonged desk work can compromise health. Physical outlets, even simple walks, counteract these effects.

- **Social connection:** Whether solitary or social, outlets can connect you with like-minded individuals who share your interests and values.

Think of your outlet as an investment in yourself—a way to recharge, reconnect, and thrive. It's not just about managing stress; it's about creating space for growth, exploration, and deeper meaning in life. Whether through creative expression, physical activity, or meaningful connections, your outlet is essential for maintaining balance and fostering personal growth.

Remember: Making time for your outlet isn't selfish—it's necessary for sustainable well-being and long-term success in all areas of life. After all, aren't you the most important person to consider.

Reflection Question: What is your outlet? What do you like to do to free your mind. Write it down and ask yourself why it matters to you.

"A good cup of tea and life are very similar. Both take time and patience. Both are to be enjoyed and savoured."

~ Life Lesson 30 ~
You Are the Masterpiece: The Centre of Your Own Universe

As we reach this final reflection, let's bring everything into perspective. While the previous lessons offer valuable tools and insights for life's journey, they all center around one crucial truth: the extraordinary nature of you.

You are far from ordinary or insignificant. In fact, you are nothing less than the center of your universe. Consider this remarkable reality: just as billions of stars illuminate the cosmos above, billions of cells orchestrate life within you. You are, in essence, a universe unto yourself and the centre point between the outer and inner universe—a unique constellation of experiences, thoughts, and potential. You entered this world as an original; never diminish yourself by becoming a copy.

Step forward with the knowledge that your life is yours to shape. You are both the artist and the masterpiece. Like any great work of art, your life's creation takes time, dedication, and clear vision. The journey of self-discovery and growth isn't meant to be rushed—it unfolds at its own perfect pace. Know that as you continue your path, there are those who believe in your potential to create something extraordinary from your life's canvas.

Remember: You were born with inherent uniqueness and infinite potential. As you move forward, hold fast to this truth. Believe in yourself, in your capacity to grow, and in your ability to create something beautiful from your experiences. Your story is still unfolding, and its next chapter awaits your touch. As stated in the first life lesson, your life is an autobiography.

Reflection Question: After all the life lessons shared and your reflections, what makes you extraordinary?...and remember, you are extraordinary!

"To sculpt a masterpiece, you must first find the right block of stone. To be a masterpiece, you must be the right block of stone."

~ Bonus Final Lesson ~
Life's Hourglass: Making Each Day Matter

Picture your life as an hourglass—each grain of sand represents a single day of your existence. At the bottom rest the days you've already lived, a collection of moments and memories from birth until now. A single grain enters a narrow chamber as you wake up each morning. Throughout the day, it gathers the experiences and people you meet - each one carrying its own story and at the end of your day, as you go to bed, that single grain falls through the narrow opening and drops below to a day that has been spent. How did you live that single grain of sand today? Did you make that grain of sand meaningful and rich?

In the upper chamber wait the days yet to come. But here lies life's great mystery: we cannot know how many grains remain. Perhaps there's just one more grain which is our last day, or maybe thousands of grains stretch before us. This uncertainty isn't meant to frighten us—it's meant to awaken us to the preciousness of each moment.

Every morning, without fail, another grain begins its descent. This is today—your gift, your opportunity, your moment to live fully. As it falls through the narrow passage, you have a choice: will this day slip by unnoticed, or will you fill it with purpose and intention? When night falls, that grain will join the others below, forever marked by how you chose to live it.

What are you doing to make today's grain count? Are you moving through your hours with meaning and gratitude? Are you seizing opportunities to grow, to connect, to contribute something significant to the world?

Each grain in your hourglass holds immense potential—not just for you, but for all whose lives you touch. This isn't about living in fear of time's passage. Rather, it's an invitation to embrace each day with purpose and appreciation. Let each grain of sand fall knowing you've lived it fully, creating ripples that extend far beyond your own hourglass.

Remember: Today's grain is falling now. How will you make it matter?

Reflection Question: Consider today, the day and moment you are reading this post. What made you smile today? What can you be grateful for today? How might you change your perspective and focus to try and focus on the positive aspects of your day?

"Time is precious – Time to change."

~ Conclusion ~
A Life Well Lived: The Final Lessons Learned

As we reach the conclusion of the life lessons shared, let us reflect on one essential truth: life's greatest wisdom often lies in simplicity. At the heart of navigating life's challenges and opportunities is the principle of *Calm and Sense*—an expression of common sense that serves as a compass when life feels uncertain or overwhelming.

In a world that consumes us with distractions, pressures, and competing priorities, staying calm is not just a luxury; it's a necessity. Calmness is the ability to pause, breathe, reflect and create a moment of clarity amidst the chaos. It empowers you to respond thoughtfully rather than react impulsively, to choose understanding over judgment, and to navigate life's storms with grace. When you cultivate calm, you invite balance into your life and gain the clarity needed to make decisions that align with your values and goals.

But calmness alone is not enough. Sense—practical wisdom, intuition, and logic—bridges the gap between reflection and action. It is about using your life experiences, values, and insights as a guide to make informed choices. Common sense isn't always common in a world that often provides complexity, but it is a deeply human tool that enables you to focus on what truly matters.

When calmness and sense work together, they create a synergy that can transform your life. Calmness clears the noise, while sense focuses the signal. Another way to consider this is that calmness provides a base for sense to emerge. Together, they help you prioritize effectively, nurture meaningful relationships, and remain grounded in a fast-paced, ever-changing world.

As you move forward, here are a few thoughts to keep with you that are threads throughout the book:

- **Pause and reflect:** Before reacting to life's demands, take a moment to center yourself. Calmness often comes from creating space between the current state and your response. Make the time to think and thank what the day held.

- **Create anchor points:** Realize your existence beyond what you do but instead, what really matters to you personally and professionally. Your anchor points will become the needle in your compass and offer you a solid grounding of where you might need to focus your attention.

- **Trust your intuition:** Your experiences and values are your guideposts. When faced with uncertainty, lean into your inner wisdom—it's often more reliable than you think. You have the tools within you to work through the hard stuff you encounter, but you need to realize and embrace that you are capable of great things.

- **Simplify Your Decisions:** The best solutions are often the simplest ones. Focus on clarity and practicality rather than overcomplicating matters.

- **Stay Balanced:** Life is a blend of challenges and joys. *Calm and Sense* help you find harmony amidst these dualities, ensuring you don't lose yourself in extremes. Find refuge in your outlet, what ever that might be, so you can focus on the tasks at hand.

In the end, *Calm and Sense* represent the art of living with intention. They remind us that wisdom is not about knowing everything but about navigating life with grace, humility, and focus. Embracing this principle is an invitation to approach life with curiosity and resilience, knowing that while you may not control every circumstance, you can always control your response.

As you continue your journey, carry the philosophy of calm and sense with you. It is the essence of common sense, a timeless guide to living a life of meaning, balance, and fulfillment.

Thank you for taking the time to read this book and allowing me to share my experiences with you. I hope these insights serve as a meaningful guide on your journey, and I wish you success and fulfillment as you navigate through your life.

Who is Sam (Ajit) Thiara

Sam (Ajit) Thiara is a distinguished educator, speaker, and mentor who has dedicated over 25 years to inspiring individuals, organizations and non-profits to realize their potential. A master storyteller and engaging facilitator, Sam seamlessly blends academic insights with practical experiences to create meaningful connections. He has delivered over 5,500 one-on-one mentorship/coaching conversations and supported 50+ non-profits which has made him a recognized leader in personal and professional development.

As Founder and the Chief Motivating Officer at his boutique organization, Ignite the Dream Coaching and Consulting, Sam focuses on individuals and organizations on critical themes around alignment, support, and growth. As a sought after and accomplished speaker, annually he delivers around 30 keynotes and workshops regionally, nationally and internationally. His signature talk, "Do You CARE (Collaboration – Adaptability – Resilience – Empathy)," resonates across industries and audiences.

Sam has authored two books and over 200 blogs, with another book in progress and a screenplay on his personal journey to India.

He holds an MA in Leadership Studies from the University of Exeter and multiple certificates from prestigious institutions, including Harvard and Stanford.

Recognized for his impactful community contributions, he is a recipient of the Governor General's Sovereign Medal for Volunteers, the Queen Elizabeth II Diamond Jubilee Medal, the King Charles III Coronation Medal and the Rick Hansen Difference Maker Medallion.

Sam's philosophy revolves around empowering others through curiosity, empathy, and the belief that every individual can uncover the extraordinary in the ordinary and lives by his signature tag line, "Everyone's life is an autobiography…make yours worth reading!"

Contact:
Website – http://www.sam-thiara.com
Email – igniting.your.dream@gmail.com or asthiara@shaw.ca
Linked In - https://www.linkedin.com/in/sthiara/

Cover design by Whitney Law

Whitney is a proud mama of two with a diverse skillset in photography, marketing, and graphic design. While she excels in many areas, she embraces the journey of growth rather than focusing on mastering a single one. Her true passion lies in connection and community.

As a BBA alumna from Simon Fraser University, Whitney's journey led her to connect with Sam Thiara, and she had the honour of designing the cover for his first book. Now, she's thrilled to be asked to design the graphic of his latest work. Combining her love for connection with her admiration for art, Whitney collaborated with her friend Sam Kaplan, whose serene nature paintings beautifully complement Sam Thiara's book - creating the perfect fusion of both their masterpieces.

Artist design by Sam Kaplan

Sam Kaplan (they/them) is a queer non-binary art maker, who is an uninvited settler on the unceded homelands of the Squamish, Musqueam, and Tsleil-Waututh People. As a city-dweller, Sam is drawn to paining moment of solitude in nature-speaking to the importance of both the preservation of and connectivity to nature.

In 2024/2025 they have had pieces exhibited through the Queer Arts Festival (The James Black Gallery), Federation of Canadian Artists, North Van Arts, Outsides and Others Gallery, Richmond Art Gallery, George Gallery, The Arts Council of Surrey Arts and Langley Arts Council.

Outside of art-making, they are a lover of growing foods, hiking, camping, and animals. In their day job they work as a counsellor and art therapist.

www.ingramcontent.com/pod-product-compliance
Lightning Source LLC
Chambersburg PA
CBHW020341010526
44119CB00048B/553